THE MOST EPIC BASEBALL STORIES FOR KIDS

Inspirational Tales of Triumph from Baseball History to Motivate Young Aspiring Champions to Score Runs and Reach for the Stars!

W. Bo Cricklewood

INTRODUCTION 7

CHAPTER 1: Swinging Through Adversity 13

    Jackie Robinson—Breaking the Color Barrier 15

    Jim Abbott—Pitching with One Hand 18

    Lesson—Courage and Perseverance 22

        • Jackie Robinson's Courage: 22

        • Jim Abbott's Perseverance: 23

    Your Turn to Shine: Leveling Up Your Courage and Perseverance 23

        • Face Your Fears, One Baby Step at a Time 23

        • Set Goals and Knock 'Em Down 24

        • Find Your Cheerleaders 25

        • Learn to Love the Word "Yet" 26

        • Practice Positive Self-Talk 26

    Taking It Beyond the Diamond 26

        • School Struggles 26

        • Sports Challenges 27

        • Personal Battles 27

        • Friend Drama 27

    Time for Some Self-Reflection 28

        1. Reflect on Your MVP (Most Valuable Perseverance) Moment 28

        2. Identify Your Current Challenge 28

        3. Create Your Game Plan 28

        4. Find Your Inner Jackie or Jim 29

        5. Celebrate Your Wins 29

CHAPTER 2: The Perfect Practice—Mastering the Fundamentals 31

    Ted Williams—The Science of Hitting 33

    Mariano Rivera—Mastering One Pitch 36

    Consistency and Specialization: What's the Deal? 39

    How Did Williams and Rivera Knock It Out of the Park? 40

        • Ted's Tactical Approach: 40

- Mariano's Mastery:..40

Your Turn to Step Up to the Plate...41

    1. Find Your Fastball:...41

    2. Practice Like a Pro:...41

    3. Break It Down:...41

    4. Embrace the Grind:...42

    5. Learn from Your Strikeouts:..42

    6. Keep a Practice Journal:..42

    7. Find Your Team:...42

    8. Set Clear Goals:...43

    9. Mix It Up (But Stay Focused):...43

    10. Rest and Recover:...43

Taking It Beyond the Diamond 43

- In School:...43

- Learning a New Skill (like coding or a musical instrument): 44

- In Your Hobbies:...44

- In Sports:..44

- In Team Projects:...45

Time for Some Self-Reflection 45

CHAPTER 3: Teamwork Makes the Dream Work 47

Derek Jeter—The Captain's Way..50

Joe Maddon—Thinking Outside the Dugout................................54

Lesson—Unity and Adaptability 58

Time to Step Up to the Plate 60

Taking It Beyond the Diamond 61

Time for Some Self-Reflection...63

CHAPTER 4: Rising to the Occasion...65

Reggie Jackson—Mr. October's Moment.....................................68

2004 Boston Red Sox—Reversing the Curse................................71

Lesson—Mental Toughness and Belief..74

Your Turn to Level Up 75

Taking It Beyond the Diamond 78

Time for Some Self-Reflection 79

CHAPTER 5: Learning From Strike Outs 81

Babe Ruth—From Mound to Moonshots 84

Chicago Cubs—A Century in the Making 87

Lesson—Adaptability and Persistence 91

Your Time to Shine 92

Taking It Beyond the Diamond 96

Time for Some Self-Reflection 97

Surprise! 98

CHAPTER 6: Game Changers 99

Hank Aaron—Hammering Through Hatred 101

Kim Ng—A New League of Her Own 103

Lesson—Resilience and Pioneering Spirit 109

Your Turn, Champ 110

Taking It Beyond the Diamond 115

Time for Some Self-Reflection 118

CONCLUSION 121

- Identify your Field: 123

- Practice, Practice, Practice: 123

- Build your Team: 124

- Embrace the Curveballs: 124

- Keep Swinging: 125

- Break Barriers: 125

INTRODUCTION

Have you ever thought baseball was just about swinging a bat and running bases? Well, slugger, you're in for a surprise bigger than a walk-off grand slam in the bottom of the ninth!

Baseball isn't just a game—it's a time machine, a life coach, and a window into America's soul, all wrapped up in a neat little package of leather and stitches. It's been the backdrop to some of the most amazing stories you'll ever hear, and trust me, these tales are gonna stick with you longer than bubble gum on a summer sidewalk.

Think of a crisp October evening. The lights are blazing, the crowd's roaring like a thunderstorm, and the air is so thick with excitement you could spread it on toast. That's baseball, champ! It's been America's favorite pastime since your great-great-grandpa was knee-high to a grasshopper! But here's where it gets really juicy. Baseball isn't just about what goes down between the foul lines. It's like a super-powered megaphone, amplifying what's happening in the world around it. Sometimes, it's even been the spark that lights the fuse of change! Baseball fever isn't just an American thing. It's gone viral, spreading from the streets of Santo Domingo to the bright lights of Seoul!

As we round the bases of this book, you're gonna rub shoulders with some of the most legendary players, teams, and moments ever to grace a diamond. We're talking about sluggers who could knock a ball into next week, pitchers who could make a baseball zigzag like a hummingbird on caffeine, and plays so unbelievable they'll have you pinching yourself to make sure you're not dreaming. Have you ever noticed how baseball and epic tales go together like hot dogs and mustard? It's no coincidence! The game is tailor-made for spinning yarns that'll keep you on the edge of your seat.

Think about it—nine innings, each one a chapter in an unfolding drama. Three strikes, building tension with every pitch. Four bases, like plot points in a story, each one bringing you closer to home. It's like baseball was designed by the world's greatest storytellers!

And here's a curveball for ya—baseball lingo isn't just for the ballpark. Ever heard someone say they "struck out" when they failed at something? Or maybe they were "thrown a curveball" when life surprised them? That's baseball sneaking into everyday chat faster than a stolen base!

But hang onto your foam finger, 'cause here comes the real magic of baseball stories: they're like a secret handshake between generations. Picture your grandma telling you about the time she saw Jackie Robinson steal home, her eyes lighting up like the scoreboard after a home run. Or your uncle describing the earthquake that shook the 1989 World Series, his voice trembling like he's still feeling the aftershocks. These stories are like time portals, zapping you straight into baseball history and making you part of something bigger than a triple-decker stadium sandwich.

So, what's on deck in this book?

You're gonna go for a ride through baseball's Hall of Fame moments! Each chapter is stuffed fuller than a catcher's mitt with stories that'll make you cheer, gasp, and maybe even get a little misty-eyed (don't sweat it, we'll say you've got dust in your eye). But these aren't just baseball stories. They're life stories, served up with a side of valuable lessons. We've scouted each tale not just because it's an all-star baseball moment, but because it's packing more wisdom than a coach with 50 years under his belt. Maybe you'll learn about never giving up from a pitcher who threw a no-hitter with one arm. Or discover the power of teamwork from a rag-tag bunch of underdogs who shocked the world. These are the kinds of stories that'll stick to your ribs long after the final out, helping you knock it out of the park in life, whether you're on the baseball diamond or tackling your math homework.

We're gonna introduce you to players who changed the game forever, like Babe Ruth, who swatted home runs like he was swatting flies, turning baseball from a ground game into an air show. Or Jackie Robinson, who didn't just break the color barrier, he smashed it to smithereens, showing the world that talent and courage come in all colors. You'll meet teams that defied the odds, like the 1969 "Miracle Mets," who went from being the laughingstock of the league to world champions faster than you can say "Play ball!" Or the 2004 Red Sox, who came back from the brink of elimination to break an 86-year-old curse, proving that it's never over 'til it's over.

And the moments?

Oh boy, the moments! We're talking about plays so incredible that they seem like they were dreamed up by a Hollywood scriptwriter with an overactive imagination. Like the time Willie Mays made a catch so incredible people are still scratching their heads over it decades later. Or when a hobbled Kirk Gibson limped to the plate in the 1988 World Series and smacked a game-winning homer that had everyone from the batboy to the hot dog vendors jumping for joy.

But it's not all fun and games (even though baseball is, you know, literally a game). We'll also dive into how baseball has been a mirror for society, reflecting the good, the bad, and the ugly of life. From the shame of segregation to the pride of Jackie Robinson breaking the color barrier, baseball has been right there in the thick of it all. We'll explore how the game has changed over the years, from the dead-ball era when home runs were as rare as a snowball in July, to today's power-packed games where the balls fly out of the park like they've got rocket boosters attached. And hey, we're not just sticking to the majors.

By the time you round third and head for home in this book, you'll have a whole new appreciation for the game. You'll see that baseball isn't just about wins and losses, home runs and strikeouts. It's about grit and determination, teamwork and individual excellence, tradition and innovation.

So, are you ready to dig in and take your cuts at the incredible world of baseball? Remember, every Major League superstar started out just like you, dreaming big and swinging for the fences.

Now, let's get this game started. Batter up!

CHAPTER 1:

Swinging Through Adversity

Ready to face some high and tight fastballs of life!

You know how sometimes it feels like the whole world's against you? Like you're trying to hit a knuckleball with your eyes closed? Well, guess what? Even the biggest baseball stars have felt that way.

This chapter is all about how the real champions don't just crush homers—they crush the curveballs life throws at them!

Think of adversity as the opposing team's ace pitcher. He's throwing everything he's got at you—sliders, changeups, and fastballs that could knock your socks off. In baseball, just like in life, you've gotta learn to hit those pitches or you'll be stuck warming the bench.

What kind of crazy pitches are we talking about here?

Well, adversity in baseball comes in all shapes and sizes. It could be facing down bullies who say you can't play because of the color of your skin. Or maybe it's trying to throw a perfect game when you've only got one hand. Heck, it could even be bouncing back after striking out with the bases loaded in the bottom of the ninth! But here's the secret—the thing that turns good players into legends. It's not about never facing adversity. It's about what you do when it comes at you like a 100 mph fastball. Do you duck and cover? Or do you dig in your cleats, keep your eye on the ball, and take your best swing?

Every single all-star you've ever heard of—from Babe Ruth to Mike Trout—has had to stare down some serious chin music. Baseball isn't just a game of hits and runs, it's a nine-inning test of guts and grit. And let me tell you, the lessons you learn on the diamond? They're the same ones that'll help you knock it out of the park in life.

In this chapter, we're gonna meet two players who didn't just face adversity—they stiff-armed it like a Hall of Fame running back and kept right on trucking to greatness. First up, we've got Jackie Robinson. He's not just playing for himself—he's playing for every kid who's ever been told they can't do something because of how they look. Then we've got Jim Abbott. Now, most pitchers have a secret weapon. Maybe it's a wicked curveball or a changeup that'll make you look sillier than a clown at a funeral. Jim's secret weapon? He learned to pitch—and pitch like a pro—with only one hand! Can you imagine trying to throw a no-hitter when you've got to switch your glove to your throwing hand after every pitch? That's like trying to catch a fly with chopsticks!

These guys didn't just face run-of-the-mill problems like a hitting slump or a sore arm. They were up against the kind of challenges that would make most people hang up their cleats and call it a day. But not Jackie and Jim. No way! They looked adversity right in the eye and said, "You call that a challenge? I call that Tuesday!" Their stories aren't just about baseball. They're about showing the world what you're made of when the chips are down. They're about standing tall when everyone's telling you to sit down. And most of all, they're about never, ever giving up on your dreams—even when it seems like your dreams have given up on you.

These incredible tales are reminders that every strikeout is a chance to learn, every error is an opportunity to improve, and every bit of adversity is just another chance to prove what you're made of.

Now, let's see how these legends turned their biggest challenges into their greatest triumphs!

Jackie Robinson—Breaking the Color Barrier

We're stepping up to the plate with Jackie Robinson, the guy who didn't just play baseball—he changed the whole dang game!

Back in 1947, baseball was as white as a fresh chalk line. Then along comes Jackie, armed with a bat, a glove, and enough guts to fill Yankee Stadium twice over. He's about to do something no African American had done since the 1880s—play in the Major Leagues. Talk about pressure!

Now, Jackie wasn't just good at baseball—he was a regular Superman in cleats! At UCLA, he didn't just play baseball. Nope, this overachiever lettered in four sports: baseball, basketball, football, and track. It's like he was trying to win a "Most Athletic Human Ever" contest! But even with all that talent, Jackie faced a wall bigger than the Green Monster in Fenway. You see, back then, baseball had this unwritten rule that said, "No African Americans Allowed." It was like having a "No Jackies" sign on every Major League clubhouse door. Then along comes Branch Rickey, the Brooklyn Dodgers' general manager. This guy had more bright ideas than Edison! He knew it was time to break baseball's color barrier, and he knew Jackie was the man to do it. But here's the kicker—he needed Jackie to promise not to fight back against all the nasty stuff that was coming his way. Can you imagine? It's like telling a catcher not to flinch when a foul tip comes screaming at his face!

On April 15, 1947, Jackie Robinson stepped onto Ebbets Field wearing Dodger blue, and boom! Just like that, baseball would never be the same. But let me tell you, it wasn't all grand slams and curtain calls. Some fans booed him louder than your dad yells at the TV during a bad call. Some players tried to spike him with their cleats—and I'm not talking about a friendly game of footsie here! Pitchers threw at his head like it was a carnival game. "Hit the Jackie, win a prize!" It was rougher than a sandpaper sandwich! But here's where Jackie showed he wasn't just a great ballplayer—he was tougher than a two-dollar steak. Remember that promise to Rickey? Jackie kept it. When players spiked him, he didn't spike 'em back. When they yelled insults, he let his bat do the talking. It's like he was playing chess while everyone else was playing checkers!

And boy, did that bat talk! Jackie played like his shoes were on fire. He stole bases like a kid grabbing cookies from the jar. He hit like he was swinging Thor's hammer instead of a Louisville Slugger. Before long, even some of the guys who'd been giving him the stink eye started to come around. Turns out talent speaks louder than prejudice—who knew?

But Jackie wasn't just changing baseball—he was changing America! He was like a human bulldozer, knocking down walls of prejudice wherever he went. Kids of all colors started dreaming of playing in the big leagues. Jackie showed everyone that talent doesn't care about the color of your skin. Jackie's impact went way beyond the ballpark. He was like a walking, talking, base-stealing Civil Rights movement! He opened doors not just for baseball players, but for all African Americans. It's like he hit a home run that flew right out of the stadium and started knocking down unfair laws all over the country!

Even after Jackie hung up his cleats, his impact kept on growing. In 1962, he became the first African American player inducted into the Baseball Hall of Fame. But Jackie wasn't done yet! He kept fighting for civil rights, using his fame to push for change. He was like a superhero who never took off his cape! In 1997, Major League Baseball did something it had never done before— it retired Jackie's number, 42, across all teams. That's right, no matter which team you root for, you'll see 42 hanging in the stadium, reminding everyone of Jackie's courage. It's like baseball's way of saying, "Thanks, Jackie, for making our game greater!"

Jackie didn't just open the door for African American players—he blew it off its hinges! After him came legends like Willie Mays, Hank Aaron, and Roberto Clemente. These guys didn't just play ball—they played it with style, flair, and sheer talent! And it wasn't just in baseball. Jackie's bravery inspired people from all walks of life. Martin Luther King Jr. once said that Jackie was "a sit-inner before sit-ins, a freedom rider before freedom rides." It's like Jackie was the leadoff hitter in the lineup of the Civil Rights movement!

So, the next time you see that number 42 hanging in a ballpark, remember Jackie Robinson. Remember the guy who didn't just play the game—he changed it. He faced down hatred with more courage than a fireman running into a burning building. And he showed us all that real strength isn't about how hard you can hit —it's about how hard you can get hit and keep moving forward.

Jackie Robinson didn't just break the color barrier—he smashed it into a million pieces. And baseball? It's been a whole lot more colorful—and a whole lot better—ever since!

Jim Abbott—Pitching with One Hand

Say hello to Jim Abbott, the pitcher who proved that when life gives you lemons, you don't just make lemonade—you use those lemons to pitch a no-hitter!

Imagine being born without a right hand in a world where most pitchers need two. That's how Jim Abbott entered the game of life. But Jim? He looked at that challenge and said, "Hold my glove... Oh wait, I'll hold it myself!" From day one, Jim was like a real-life superhero with a unique superpower—the ability to turn what some saw as a weakness into his greatest strength. It's like he had a secret identity: mild-mannered Jim Abbott by day, pitching sensation by... well, also the day, because baseball games are usually during the day. You get the point!

Jim's baseball journey started in Little League, where he first showed the world he wasn't just going to play—he was going to dominate! While other kids were trying to remember which hand their glove went on, Jim was developing a technique smoother than a freshly groomed infield. He would pitch with his left hand, then faster than you can say "Holy Smokes, Batman!", he'd slip his glove onto his left hand to field. It was like watching a magician, only instead of pulling rabbits out of hats, he was pulling off impossible plays! In high school, Jim wasn't just good —he was throw-a-no-hitter-in-the-state-championship-game good! That's right, while most high schoolers are worrying about prom dates, Jim was busy making batters look sillier than a clown at a 50th birthday party. But Jim wasn't just a baseball star. Oh no, this overachiever was also the quarterback of the football team and a point guard in basketball.

Now, let's break down Jim's pitching technique. He'd hold his glove on the end of his right arm. After throwing the pitch, he'd smoothly slip his left hand into the glove, ready to field. Then, if he needed to throw to a base, he'd slip the glove under his right arm, grab the ball with his left hand, and fire it off. This technique wasn't only clever—it was smooth! Jim could pitch, catch, and throw to first base faster than most two-handed pitchers. It was like he had baseball superpowers!

Jim's talent took him all the way to the 1988 Olympics, where he pitched Team USA to a gold medal. It's like he said, "A gold medal? Don't mind if I do!" But Jim was just getting started. After the Olympics, Jim went straight to the major leagues without even stopping in the minors. That's like skipping from kindergarten straight to college! In his first season with the California Angels, he won 12 games and finished fifth in the Rookie of the Year voting. Not too shabby for a rookie, eh?

But hold onto your baseball caps, because the best is yet to come. On September 4, 1993, Jim Abbott threw a no-hitter for the New York Yankees. A no-hitter! That's like pitching a perfect game in a video game, except this was real life! Imagine the scene: Yankee Stadium, packed to the rafters. The crowd's so quiet you could hear a hot dog wrapper drop. Jim's on the mound, cool as a cucumber. He winds up, he pitches... and batters are swinging and missing so much, you'd think the ball was invisible! Nine innings later, history is made. Jim Abbott, the guy they said couldn't pitch in the majors, just threw a no-hitter. It's like he looked at impossible and said, "That's cute. Hold my Gatorade."

Jim's impact went way beyond the baseball diamond. He became a hero to millions of kids (and adults) who faced their own challenges. It was like he was saying, "Hey, if I can pitch in the major leagues with one hand, what's stopping you from chasing your dreams?" He didn't just inspire people with disabilities—he inspired everyone. He showed the world that it's not about what you don't have, it's about what you do with what you've got. He turned "You can't" into "Just watch me!"

After hanging up his cleats, Jim didn't ride off into the sunset. Nope, he became a motivational speaker, spreading his message of determination and positivity faster than a fastball. He's written books, given speeches, and continues to inspire people to overcome their own challenges. Jim's story teaches us that the only real disability in life is a bad attitude. He's living proof that when life throws you a curveball, you can either strike out or knock it out of the park.

Jim? He chose to swing for the fences every single time. His legacy in baseball is huge, but his impact off the field might be even bigger. He's shown countless people that their perceived limitations don't define them. Schools have used Jim's story to teach kids about perseverance. Sports teams at all levels have invited him to speak about overcoming obstacles. And parents of kids with disabilities often share Jim's story as a beacon of hope and possibility.

So, the next time you're facing a challenge that seems bigger than a mountain, remember Jim Abbott. Remember the guy who looked at what most people would call a disability and said, "Nah, that's my power." He didn't just play the game—he changed the rules, inspired millions, and showed us all that anything is possible if you've got the heart, the hustle, and the willingness to try.

Jim Abbott didn't just pitch with one hand—he single-handedly proved that the human spirit is stronger than any obstacle. Now that's what I call a true all-star!

Lesson—Courage and Perseverance

So what turned Jackie Robinson and Jim Abbott from regular Joes into baseball legends? It's straight-up courage and perseverance—the dynamic duo of success that'll help you knock life's curveballs out of the park!

Now what exactly is the big deal with courage and perseverance?

First up, let's crack open the dictionary of awesomeness and define these superpower words:

- **Courage:** It's facing your fears head-on, even when your knees are shaking like a leaf in a hurricane. It's standing up for what's right, even when it feels like the whole world is giving you the stink eye.

- **Perseverance:** This is sticking to your guns when things get tough. It's like being a human boomerang—no matter how many times life throws you away, you keep coming back!

In the world of sports and life, courage and perseverance are like peanut butter and jelly—they just belong together!

Now, let's look at how our baseball buddies, Jackie Robinson and Jim Abbott, rocked these qualities like they were going out of style.

- **Jackie Robinson's Courage:**
  - Faced crowds booing louder than your dad when the ref makes a bad call
  - Dealt with other players trying to hurt him just because of his skin color

- Kept his cool when others tried to rattle him (imagine trying to hit a home run while someone was yelling in your ear!)

- Stood tall and played his heart out, changing the game forever

- **Jim Abbott's Perseverance:**
  - Born without a right hand, but didn't let that stop him from becoming a pitcher

  - Invented a new way to pitch and field that worked for him

  - Kept pushing and practicing when others doubted him

  - Pitched a no-hitter in the major leagues (that's like getting every answer right on a pop quiz!)

These guys didn't just play baseball—they rewrote the rulebook on what's possible when you've got courage and perseverance in your dugout!

Your Turn to Shine: Leveling Up Your Courage and Perseverance

"That's great for Jackie and Jim, but how do I get me some of that courage and perseverance?"

Well, young winner, here are some strategies that'll make you braver than a firefighter and more persistent than a telemarketer!

- **Face Your Fears, One Baby Step at a Time**

  Courage isn't about not being scared—it's about being scared and doing it anyway! It's all about making gradual progress, like climbing a staircase—one step at a time. When you start small, you build momentum for the bigger challenges.

- ○ Start small. Scared of public speaking? Start by raising your hand in class. For instance:

    - Start small: low stakes, high reward.

    - Build up: Offer to speak in front of a small group, like a book club or a team huddle.

    - Go bigger: Volunteer for a presentation. It doesn't have to be a TED Talk—just a step up from where you started.

    - Keep growing: Each time, push yourself a bit more until, before you know it, you're commanding the room like a boss.

- ○ Before you know it, you'll be giving speeches like you're running for President!

- **Set Goals and Knock 'Em Down**

    Perseverance loves a good goal. Goals are your compass, guiding you toward progress. But the trick is to break them down into snack-sized bite.

    - ○ Example: Setting SMART Goals

        - S (Specific): Instead of "I want to get better at baseball," try, "I want to improve my batting average by 10% in the next three months."

        - M (Measurable): Keep track of your progress—write it down, track those batting stats, or use a checklist.

- A (Achievable): Don't aim to go from rookie to MVP overnight. Focus on realistic improvements.

- R (Relevant): Make sure your goal fits your overall life goals, whether that's becoming a better athlete or just having fun.

- T (Time-Bound): Set a deadline, like three months, to create urgency and accountability.

○ Each little victory will fuel you for the next challenge.

○ Soon, you'll be taking on goals bigger than Babe Ruth's appetite!

- **Find Your Cheerleaders**

Surround yourself with people who believe in you more than you believe in yourself.

○ They're like your personal pep squad, ready to boost you up when you're feeling down.

○ These could be friends, family, or teammates—anyone who lifts you up.

○ Don't be shy about asking for encouragement or advice when you're feeling down.

○ Cheer them on when they need it, too! It builds a positive loop of support.

○ Don't have a cheerleader? Be your own! Look in the mirror and give yourself a pep talk.

- **Learn to Love the Word "Yet"**

  Adding "yet" to the end of your doubts turns obstacles into stepping stones. Suddenly, you're not failing—you're on your way.

  - When you face a setback, add "yet" to the end of your "I can't" statements.

    - "I can't hit a curveball... yet." "I can't solve these math problems... yet."

  - It's like magic—suddenly, failure becomes a pit stop on the road to success!

- **Practice Positive Self-Talk**

  - Being your own biggest fan isn't cheesy—it's necessary! That voice inside your head? It needs to sound more like your own personal hype man.

    - Instead of saying, "I'm gonna mess this up," try, "I've got this!"

  - Imagine having a tiny Jackie Robinson or Jim Abbott on your shoulder, cheering you on.

Taking It Beyond the Diamond

Now, let's take these lessons and apply them to your life faster than a Jackie Robinson stolen base!

- **School Struggles**

  Maybe you're having a tough time with math. Instead of throwing in the towel, channel your inner Jim Abbott. Break down those equations like Jim broke down his pitching technique.

○ Practice, adjust, and keep swinging until you hit a home run in your next test!

- **Sports Challenges**

Didn't make the team? Feeling like you're in a slump? Remember Jackie Robinson. He faced challenges way tougher than a batting slump, and he kept his cool and let his skills do the talking.

○ Stay focused, keep practicing, and show 'em what you're made of!

- **Personal Battles**

Dealing with bullies or feeling like you don't fit in? Take a page from both Jackie and Jim's playbooks.

○ Stand tall like Jackie, knowing that your character is worth more than any insult.

○ And like Jim, focus on your strengths. You've got talents that make you unique—let them shine!

- **Friend Drama**

Friendships can be trickier than a knuckleball sometimes. When things get tough, think about how Jackie and Jim handled adversity.

○ Be brave enough to stand up for yourself or others, and persistent enough to work through problems instead of giving up on good friends.

Time for Some Self-Reflection

Now it's time for some homework—but don't worry, this is the fun kind!

1. Reflect on Your MVP (Most Valuable Perseverance) Moment

Think about a time when you faced a challenge. Maybe you bombed a test, struck out in a big game, or had a fight with your best friend.

a. How did you handle it? Did you show courage? Perseverance? Both?

b. Give yourself a high five for getting through it!

2. Identify Your Current Challenge

a. What's a challenge you're facing right now?

b. How can you tackle it with the courage of Jackie Robinson and the perseverance of Jim Abbott?

c. Maybe it's finally talking to your crush (courage alert!), or working on that book report you've been putting off (perseverance to the rescue!).

3. Create Your Game Plan

Write down three specific actions you can take to face your challenge.

a. **Example:** If you're struggling with a subject in school, your plan might be:

   i. Ask your teacher for extra help

   ii. Form a study group with friends

iii. Practice problems for 15 minutes every day

4. Find Your Inner Jackie or Jim

When you're feeling down or discouraged, ask yourself: "What would Jackie do?" or "How would Jim handle this?"

a. Use their stories as inspiration to keep pushing forward.

5. Celebrate Your Wins

Every time you show courage or perseverance, no matter how small, celebrate it!

a. Keep a "Victory Journal" where you write down your daily acts of bravery and persistence.

b. Before you know it, you'll have a whole book of your own legendary moments!

You've got more strength inside you than you know. Here's the real secret—courage and perseverance aren't just for baseball diamonds or history books. They're your ticket to crushing it in the game of life! Every time you stand up for yourself or someone else, that's a Jackie Robinson moment. Every time you keep trying when things get tough, that's a Jim Abbott pitch.

You might not be breaking baseball's color barrier or pitching a no-hitter with one hand, but your challenges are just as real and just as important. You've got courage. You've got perseverance.

Now get out there and knock it out of the park!

CHAPTER 2:

The Perfect Practice— Mastering the Fundamentals

You know that old saying, "Practice makes perfect"? Well, in baseball, it's more like "Perfect practice makes perfect."

We're not just talking about mindlessly tossing a ball around. Nope, we're diving into the kind of practice that makes your muscles remember the moves even when your brain is daydreaming about post-game pizza! Think about it like this: Baseball practice is like being a mad scientist, but instead of mixing chemicals, you're experimenting with your swing, your pitch, your catch. You try something, see how it works, then tweak it until it's juuuust right. It's like fine-tuning a race car, except the race car is you!

"But I'm already pretty good at baseball. Do I really need to practice that much?"

Let me tell you something, hotshot. Even the greatest players who ever stepped on a diamond—guys who seemed like they were born with a bat in their hands—they practiced like their lives depended on it. You see, practice isn't just about getting better. It's about getting so good that when the pressure's on, when the crowd's roaring and the game's on the line, your body knows exactly what to do without you even having to think about it. It's not about how many hours you spend on the field. It's about how you spend those hours. Quality over quantity, champs! One hour of super-focused, laser-beam practice can be worth more than a whole day of just going through the motions.

In this chapter, we're going to meet two baseball superheroes who took practice to a whole new level. First up, we've got Ted Williams, the "Splendid Splinter" himself. This guy was so obsessed with perfecting his swing that he'd practice until his hands bled! Talk about dedication! Then we've got Mariano Rivera, the "Sandman," the greatest closer in baseball history. This dude threw basically one pitch his entire career. But man, did he practice that pitch until it was more unhittable than a mosquito on a motorcycle!

These guys didn't just practice; they turned practice into an art form. They analyzed every tiny detail, adjusted every little thing, and prepared their minds like Jedi masters. And the result? They didn't just play baseball—they dominated it!

So get ready, because we're about to learn how to practice like the pros!

Alright, sluggers! Let's dive into two of baseball's heaviest hitters (in more ways than one) and see how they knocked it out of the park when it came to practice and dedication. We're talking about Ted Williams and Mariano Rivera - two guys who took different paths but ended up in the same place: Baseball legendville. Buckle up, because this is gonna be one heck of a ride!

Ted Williams—The Science of Hitting

So, it's the 1940s, and while most guys are swinging away hoping to connect with the ball, there's one dude in Boston who's treating the batter's box like it's a science lab.

That's right, we're talking about Ted Williams, the guy who turned hitting a baseball into a full-blown science project—and man, did he get results!

- **The obsession begins:** Ted wasn't just interested in hitting—he was obsessed. We're talking "stay up all night thinking about it" obsessed. "Practice until your hands bleed" obsessed. This guy ate, slept, and breathed hitting.

- **The bab rat:** Williams didn't just practice—he experimented. He'd spend hours watching pitches, studying how the ball moved, figuring out the best way to connect. It was like he was trying to crack some secret code that only he could see.

- **The book that changed the game:** In 1971, Williams dropped a bomb on the baseball world—his book "The Science of Hitting." This wasn't just any old baseball book. It was like the hitting Bible. In it, Williams broke down everything—from the physics of a swing to the psychology of facing a pitcher. He even included a chart showing exactly where he hit best in the strike zone. Talk about giving away your secrets!

- **Practice makes perfect... then practice some more:** Williams didn't just talk the talk—he walked the walk. Or should we say, he swung the swing? This guy practiced like his life depended on it. He'd spend hours in the batting cage, tweaking his swing, trying to get it just right. And when he thought he had it perfect? He'd practice some more.

- **The results speak for themselves:** All this obsession, all this practice—did it pay off? You bet your baseball cards it did! Williams ended his career with a .344 batting average. For you non-baseball folks, that's like acing every test you ever took... for 19 years straight!

- **Never stop learning:** Here's the kicker—even when Williams was at the top of his game, he never stopped trying to improve. He was always watching, always learning, always trying to get better. It's like he had this burning desire to unlock every secret baseball had to offer.

- **The vision thing:** Williams wasn't just gifted with a great swing—he had eyes like a hawk. He could see the seams on a baseball coming at him at 90 miles per hour. How? Practice, baby! He'd spend hours just watching pitches, training his eyes to pick up the tiniest details.

- **The mental game:** But it wasn't all about the physical stuff. Williams knew that hitting was just as much a mental game as a physical one. He studied pitchers like they were textbooks, learning their habits, their tells, anything that could give him an edge.

- **Sharing the knowledge:** Here's where Williams really shines —he didn't keep all this knowledge to himself. He became one of the most respected hitting coaches in the game, sharing his insights with younger players. It's like he was creating an army of mini-Ted Williamses!

- **The legacy:** Even today, decades after Williams hung up his bat, his approach to hitting is still influencing players. His book is like required reading for serious hitters. It's proof that when you combine raw talent with obsessive study and practice, you can change the game forever.

So, what can we learn from Ted Williams? A few key things:

- Passion isn't just about loving something—it's about dedicating yourself to understanding it completely.

- There's always room for improvement, even when you're at the top of your game.

- Knowledge is power—and sharing that knowledge can create a lasting legacy.

Ted Williams didn't just play baseball—he studied it, he lived it, he breathed it. He turned hitting into a science, and in doing so, he didn't just become one of the greatest hitters of all time—he changed the way we think about the game itself.

Whether it's baseball or anything else in life, if you want to be the best, you've got to be willing to put in the work. Study hard, practice harder, and never stop trying to improve.

Mariano Rivera—Mastering One Pitch

Let's switch gears and talk about a guy who took a completely different approach to baseball greatness.

While Ted Williams was out there trying to master every aspect of hitting, Mariano Rivera was focused on one thing and one thing only: throwing the perfect pitch. And boy, did he nail it!

- **The unlikely beginning:** Picture this—a skinny kid from Panama shows up to his first pro tryout wearing a borrowed glove and shoes that don't even fit. Sounds like the start of a bad sports movie, right? Nope, it's the beginning of Mariano Rivera's journey to becoming the greatest closer in baseball history.

- **The discovery:** Rivera started out as a so-so starting pitcher. But then, during a game of catch in 1997, something magical happened. Rivera threw a pitch that moved like it had a mind of its own. It was the cut fastball—or "cutter"—and it was about to change everything.

- **The decision:** Now, most pitchers would've been happy to add this new pitch to their arsenal. But Rivera? He decided to go all in. He wasn't just going to throw the cutter—he was going to master it. It was like he'd found his superpower, and he was determined to become a superhero.

- **Practice, practice, and more practice:** Rivera's dedication to perfecting the cutter was off the charts. We're talking thousands of throws, day after day, year after year. He'd throw it in the bullpen, during warmups, in games. If Rivera was awake, chances are he was thinking about or throwing his cutter.

- **The science of one pitch:** Like Williams with hitting, Rivera turned his pitch into a science. He studied how it moved, how batters reacted to it, and how it behaved in different weather conditions. He wasn't just throwing a pitch—he was conducting an ongoing experiment.

- **The results:** All this focus on one pitch paid off big time. Rivera's cutter became legendary. Batters knew it was coming, and they still couldn't hit it. It was like trying to hit a mosquito with a toothpick—in the dark!

- **Consistency is key:** Here's where Rivera really shines. He didn't just have a few good seasons—he was dominant for nearly two decades. From 1997 to his retirement in 2013, he was the most feared closer in baseball. That's like being the best at anything for 16 years straight!

- **Mental toughness:** But it wasn't just about the physical act of throwing the pitch. Rivera had nerves of steel. Closers only come in during the most high-pressure situations, and Rivera thrived on it. It was like the bigger the moment, the better he got.

- **The legacy:** Rivera retired with a career ERA of 2.21 and 652 saves. For you non-baseball folks, that's like getting an A+ on every test for your entire school career. He was so good that the Yankees retired his number (42) and he became the first player ever unanimously voted into the Hall of Fame.

- **Sharing the knowledge:** Like Williams, Rivera didn't keep his secrets to himself. He became known as a mentor to younger pitchers, sharing his insights and experiences. It's like he was passing on the torch, ensuring his legacy would live on through the next generation.

So, what can we learn from Mariano Rivera? A few key things:

- Sometimes, being the best at one thing is better than being good at many things.

- Consistency and reliability can be just as impressive as flashy performances.

- Mental strength is just as important as physical skill, especially under pressure.

Mariano Rivera didn't try to be the best at everything—he focused on being the absolute best at one thing. And in doing so, he didn't just become a great player—he became a legend.

Here's the takeaway, champs: Whether you're like Ted Williams, trying to master every aspect of your craft, or like Mariano Rivera, focusing on perfecting one specific skill, the key is dedication. Find what you're passionate about, work at it relentlessly, and never stop trying to improve.

Greatness doesn't happen overnight. It's the result of years of hard work, countless hours of practice, and an unwavering commitment to being the best you can be. Whether you're on the baseball diamond or in the classroom, channel your inner Williams or Rivera. Focus, practice, and stay consistent.

Speaking of consistency, it's time to step up to the plate and talk about two of the biggest game-changers in baseball: consistency and specialization. We've seen how Ted Williams and Mariano Rivera knocked it out of the park with these skills, but now it's your turn to swing for the fences in your own life. Let's break it down!

Consistency and Specialization: What's the Deal?

Well, well, well, let's kick off by understanding what these two words mean.

- **Consistency:** Think of this as your everyday hustle. It's showing up, day in and day out, rain or shine, and giving it your all. In baseball terms, it's like hitting .300 every single season, not just when you feel like it. It's that steady grind that helps you get better at whatever you're working on, whether it's learning to do a handstand or acing those math problems.

- **Specialization:** This is all about finding your superpower and cranking it up to 11. It's like being the best cleanup hitter or having the nastiest curveball in the league. You're not trying to be okay at a bunch of stuff—you want to be awesome at that one thing.

How Did Williams and Rivera Knock It Out of the Park?

- **Ted's Tactical Approach:**
  - Williams treated hitting like a full-time job... and then some! He didn't just practice—he studied. Every pitch, every swing, every at-bat was a chance to learn.
  - He broke hitting down into a science, analyzing every little detail. It's like he was solving a baseball equation every time he stepped up to the plate.
  - Even when he was already great, he kept pushing to be better. That's consistency, folks!

- **Mariano's Mastery:**
  - Rivera took one pitch—the cutter—and made it his whole world. He didn't need a dozen different pitches. He had one, and he made sure it was unhittable.
  - Day after day, year after year, Rivera threw that cutter. He didn't get bored. He didn't switch it up. He just kept refining and perfecting his craft.

○ When the game was on the line, everyone knew what was coming. But knowing and hitting are two different things!

Your Turn to Step Up to the Plate

So, how can you take these lessons and apply them to your own life? Whether you're trying to ace your math test or become the next YouTube star, here are some strategies to help you hit a home run:

1. Find Your Fastball:

a. What's something you love and are really good at? Maybe it's singing, coding, or soccer. Find that thing and make it your focus.

b. Don't try to do everything. If you're good at baking cookies, don't also try to become a guitar master at the same time. Focus on becoming unstoppable at that one thing.

2. Practice Like a Pro:

a. Set a schedule and stick to it. Maybe it's 30 minutes, even 15 minutes, a day or two hours every weekend.

b. The key is consistency. A little bit every day beats a lot once in a while. Like brushing your teeth!

3. Break It Down:

a. Take a page from Ted Williams' book and analyze your skill. What parts can you improve?

b. What are the components? How can you improve each one? If you're learning guitar, maybe focus on chords one day, then rhythm the next. Little improvements stack up over time.

4. Embrace the Grind:

a. Remember Rivera throwing the same pitch over and over? You've gotta get used to the repetition. It's okay if it feels boring sometimes—that's where the magic happens!

b. It might get boring, but that's where the magic happens. Push through and keep going!

5. Learn from Your Strikeouts:

a. Every failure is a chance to learn. Don't get discouraged —get curious!

b. Ask yourself: What went wrong? How can I do better next time? Failures are just lessons in disguise.

6. Keep a Practice Journal:

a. Track your progress. What's working? What isn't? Start a journal. Write down what you're working on, what's going well, and where you can improve.

b. Celebrate your progress, even the small stuff! Scored a goal? Nailed that tricky piano piece? Write it down! Every step forward counts!

7. Find Your Team:

a. Surround yourself with people who support your goals.

b. Maybe it's a study group or a coding club. Whatever it is, find your tribe!

8. Set Clear Goals:

a. What's your World Series? Maybe it's getting an A in math, or hitting a home run. Define what success looks like for you.

b. Break it down into smaller goals. What's your next base? Break it down into smaller goals, like "study for 20 minutes a day," or "practice my swing." Step by step, you'll get closer to your "World Series" moment.

9. Mix It Up (But Stay Focused):

a. Even Rivera practiced other pitches to keep his arm strong. You can mix it up a bit too! If you're a basketball player, maybe practice dribbling, but don't forget about your shooting.

b. But remember—always stay focused on your main goal.

10. Rest and Recover:

a. Even the best players need a day off.

b. Make sure you're getting enough sleep and taking care of yourself.

Taking It Beyond the Diamond

Now, let's see how these lessons can knock it out of the park in other areas of life:

- **In School:**
  - Find your "subject superpower" and really dive deep into it.

- Set a consistent study schedule. A little bit every day beats cramming!

- Break down big projects into smaller tasks, just like breaking down a swing.

- **Learning a New Skill (like coding or a musical instrument):**

  - Focus on mastering the fundamentals before moving on to advanced stuff.

  - Practice consistently, even if it's just for 15 minutes a day.

  - Analyze your progress and adjust your approach as needed.

- **In Your Hobbies:**

  - Identify what aspect of your hobby you enjoy most and specialize in it.

  - Set regular practice times and stick to them.

  - Keep track of your improvement and celebrate your progress.

- **In Sports:**

  - Choose one skill to focus on, like shooting, dribbling, or passing.

  - Set a practice schedule—maybe 15 minutes every day after school.

  - Track your progress by keeping a chart of your scores or improvements.

- **In Team Projects:**
  - Discuss everyone's strengths at the beginning of the project.
  - Assign specific tasks that align with each person's skills.
  - Check in regularly to support each other and make adjustments if needed.

Time for Some Self-Reflection

Champs, it's time to take a good look at your own practice routine. Grab a pen and paper (or your phone, we're not judging) and answer these questions:

1. What's your "cutter"? What skill do you want to master?

2. How often are you currently practicing? Is it consistent?

3. Are you analyzing your performance and looking for ways to improve?

4. What's one small change you can make to your routine to be more like Williams or Rivera?

5. Who's on your "team"? Who can support and encourage you?

Remember, becoming great at something doesn't happen overnight. It's about showing up day after day, putting in the work, and staying focused on your goals. Williams and Rivera didn't become legends by accident—they made a choice to be the best and then backed it up with hard work and dedication.

So, what's it gonna be, champ? Are you ready to step up to the plate and swing for the fences in your own life? Whether you're aiming to be the Ted Williams of math class or the Mariano Rivera of guitar playing, the principles are the same: find your strength, practice consistently, and never stop trying to improve.

You've got the bat in your hands now. It's your turn to write your own legend—every great player started as a rookie.

CHAPTER 3:

Teamwork Makes the Dream Work

It's time to huddle up and talk about something that's as important in baseball as a well-oiled glove or a perfectly balanced bat. We're diving into Chapter 3: Teamwork Makes the Dream Work!

"Wait a second, isn't baseball all about those epic home runs and jaw-dropping catches?"

Well, sure, those highlight reels are awesome, but here's the solid secret: behind every amazing play is a team working together like a well-oiled machine. It's like a baseball symphony, with every player hitting their note at just the right time!

Imagine it's the bottom of the ninth, bases loaded, two outs, and your team is down by one. The batter steps up to the plate, cool as a cucumber. But how did we get here? It wasn't just that one player. It was the pitcher who threw six solid innings, the reliever who got out of a jam in the seventh, the outfielder who made a diving catch in the eighth, and the players who got on base before our hero stepped up. That's teamwork, folks!

Behind every great team is a leader who can rally the troops when the chips are down. Think of them as the conductor of our baseball orchestra. They're the ones who can look a player in the eye and say, "You've got this," and make them believe it. They're the glue that holds the team together when things get tough.

"Why should I care about teamwork and leadership? I just want to hit dingers!"

Here's the scoop: understanding how to work as a team and lead others isn't just about winning baseball games (although that's pretty awesome). These are powers you can use everywhere in life!

Imagine you're working on a group project at school. Suddenly, all that practice communicating with your teammates on the field pays off. You know how to listen to others, share your ideas, and work together to create something amazing. Or maybe you're organizing a fundraiser for your local animal shelter. All those times you helped rally your team when you were down by three runs? That experience helps you inspire others to join your cause.

In this chapter, we're going to meet two All-Stars of teamwork and leadership: Derek Jeter and Joe Maddon. These guys are like the Batman and Superman of baseball teamwork (but don't ask me which is which—that's a debate for another day!).

First up, we've got Derek Jeter. This guy wasn't just a shortstop— he was a captain, a leader, and the heart and soul of the New York Yankees for 20 years! Jeter wasn't always the one hitting the most home runs or having the highest batting average, but he had something special: he knew how to bring out the best in his teammates. He led by example, always giving 110% whether his team was up by 10 or down by 9. Jeter was the guy who could make a rookie feel like an All-Star and remind a veteran why they loved the game. He was like the peanut butter that held the Yankees sandwich together!

Then we've got Joe Maddon, the Merlin of baseball managers. This guy could take a team of underdogs and turn them into world beaters! Maddon wasn't your typical "by the book" manager. Oh no, he was more like the guy who threw the book out and wrote his own—probably with crayons and lots of pictures! He knew that to get the best out of his players, he had to keep things fun and relaxed. Dress-up road trips? Check. Petting zoos in the clubhouse? Why not! But don't let the funny stuff fool you—when it came to strategy and getting his team to play as one, Maddon was as serious as a fastball to the ribs.

So, why are we shining the spotlight on these two? Because Jeter and Maddon show us that there's more than one way to lead a team to victory. Jeter was the quiet leader, the guy who showed everyone how it's done by doing it himself. Maddon was the out-of-the-box thinker, the guy who knew that a happy team is a winning team. But both of them understood the secret sauce of baseball success: it's not just about having nine great players—it's about having nine players working together as one unstoppable force!

As we explore their stories, keep your eyes peeled for the little things. How did Jeter pump up his teammates without saying a word? How did Maddon turn a bunch of individual players into a family? And most importantly, how can you take these lessons and use them in your own life?

Remember, whether you're on the baseball diamond, in the classroom, or just hanging out with your friends, the skills of teamwork and leadership are your ticket to the big leagues of life. So let's learn from the best!

Derek Jeter—The Captain's Way

Alright, team! Let's talk about a guy who could make pinstripes look cooler than a superhero cape. We're diving into the epic world of Derek Jeter, the captain of the New York Yankees and the guy who made playing shortstop look easier than eating hot dogs at a ballgame!

- **The making of a captain:** It's 1995, and a skinny kid from Kalamazoo, Michigan, steps onto the field at Yankee Stadium. Fast forward a few years, and that same kid is being handed the captain's armband. That's Derek Jeter for you—

going from rookie to leader faster than you can say "World Series ring"!

- **Leading without a megaphone:** Now, Jeter wasn't your typical rah-rah, in-your-face kind of leader. Nope, he was more like a baseball ninja. He didn't need to shout to be heard. His actions spoke louder than any pep talk ever could.

- **The Jeter Jump Throw:** This wasn't just a cool move—it was a statement. It said, "Hey team, check this out. I'm giving 110% on every play, and you should too!"

- **The Clutch Gene:** When the game was on the line, Jeter didn't sweat. He thrived. It was like he had ice in his veins and fire in his bat.

- **The calm in the storm:** Yankees in a slump? Jeter kept his cool. Media frenzy? Jeter stayed focused. It was like watching a duck on water—calm on the surface, paddling like crazy underneath.

  - **Jeter's secret—consistency:** You know how some players are hot one day and cold the next? Not Jeter. He was like your favorite pizza place—reliably good, day in and day out.

  - **Mr. Dependable:** Whether it was April or October, Jeter brought his A-game. It was like he had a "No Bad Days" policy.

  - **The eyes have it:** Jeter's teammates knew one look from him could say it all. A nod here, a glance there—it was like he had baseball telepathy!

- **Practice makes perfect:** Jeter wasn't just talented - he worked his socks off. First to arrive, last to leave. It was like he was allergic to slacking.

  o **The Jeter Effect:** Jeter didn't just play the game—he changed it. And he didn't just lead a team—he inspired a generation.

  o **The Rookie Whisperer:** New guy on the team? Jeter took them under his wing faster than you can say "Yankees Universe."

  o **The Clubhouse Glue:** Arguments? Tension? Not on Jeter's watch. He kept the team tighter than a well-oiled glove.

- **The Face of Baseball:** Jeter wasn't just a Yankee—he was Mr. Baseball. Kids wanted to be him, players wanted to play like him.

  o **Clutch performance? That's just another Tuesday for Jeter:** Some players crumble under pressure. Jeter? He ate pressure for breakfast.

  o **The Flip Play:** 2001 playoffs against Oakland. Jeter comes out of nowhere to make an impossible play. It wasn't in the playbook—it was pure Jeter magic.

  o **Mr. November:** 2001 World Series, Game 4. Clock strikes midnight, making it November 1st. Jeter hits a walk-off home run. Talk about writing your own fairy tale!

  o **3000th hit? Make it a homer:** Most players would be happy with a single for their 3000th hit. Jeter? He goes yard. Because of course he does.

- **More than just a player:** Jeter wasn't just about what happened between the foul lines. He was a pro's pro, on and off the field.

  - **The Derek Jeter Turn 2 Foundation:** Giving back to the community? Check. Jeter was as clutch with charity as he was with batting.

  - **Media Maestro:** In the Big Apple's pressure cooker, Jeter never cracked. He handled the press like he handled a ground ball—smoothly and without error.

- **Role model supreme:** In an era of scandals, Jeter kept his nose clean. Kids could look up to him without their parents having to worry.

  - **The Jeter Legacy:** When Jeter hung up his cleats, he left more than just stats in the record books.

  - **The intangibles:** Leadership, clutch performance, consistency—Jeter wrote the book on baseball intangibles.

  - **The standard:** Being a Yankee meant something special because of guys like Jeter. He set the bar sky-high.

  - **The memories:** From the jump throw to the dive into the stands, Jeter gave fans a highlight reel of memories.

So, what can we learn from The Captain? A few key things:

- Actions speak louder than words. You don't need to shout to be a leader.

- Consistency is key. Bring your A-game every day, not just when you feel like it.

- Pressure is a privilege. The biggest moments are your chance to shine.

- It's not just about you. True leaders make everyone around them better.

Derek Jeter was an entire baseball experience. He showed us that being a leader isn't about having the loudest voice or the flashiest plays. It's about showing up, day in and day out, and giving everything you've got.

So whether it's a tough game or a hard test, ask yourself: "What would Jeter do?" Chances are, the answer is: Stay cool, work hard, and come through when it counts. That's the Captain's way, and it's a pretty good way to live, on and off the field.

Remember, you might not have Jeter's jump throw, but you can definitely have his attitude.

Joe Maddon—Thinking Outside the Dugout

Let's talk about a guy who makes mad scientists look boring. We're diving into the wacky, wonderful world of Joe Maddon, the manager who turned baseball strategy on its head and had more tricks up his sleeve than a magician at a birthday party!

- **The Maddon Method:** Imagine walking into a baseball clubhouse and seeing... a petting zoo? Or your manager dressed like a hippie? Welcome to Joe Maddon's world, where "normal" is just a setting on a washing machine!

  - **Saberme-what?:** While other managers were stuck in the Stone Age, Maddon was all about the numbers. Analytics? He ate that stuff for breakfast!

- **The Lineup Shuffle:** Pitcher batting 8th? Leadoff hitter in the 9 spot? With Maddon, the only rule was there are no rules!

- **Shifting gears:** Maddon's defensive shifts were so extreme, they made the Grand Canyon look like a pothole. He'd put his fielders in places that made you think, "Is he watching the same game we are?"

- **Chemistry 101 with Professor Maddon:** Maddon didn't just manage a team—he created a family. And like any good family, his had its fair share of weird traditions!

  - **Dress-up days:** Road trip? More like a fashion show! Maddon had his teams dressing up in everything from disco outfits to superhero costumes. Who says baseball can't be fabulous?

  - **Clubhouse critters:** Penguins, flamingos, even a python! Maddon's clubhouse was part locker room, part zoo. Talk about team bonding!

  - **The Maddon Motto:** "Try Not to Suck" became the Cubs' rallying cry. It was like the world's most honest pep talk!

- **Breaking the Billy Goat Curse:** 108 years! That's how long Cubs fans waited for a World Series win. Enter Joe Maddon, the curse-breaker extraordinaire!

  - **Building belief:** Maddon didn't just manage a team - he managed expectations. He made Cubs fans believe the impossible was possible.

- **Pressure? What pressure?:** When the whole world was watching, Maddon kept things loose. It was like he had a PhD in Chill.

- **The Rain Delay speech:** Game 7 of the World Series, tied game, rain delay. Maddon gathers the team and... cracks jokes? That's right, keeping it light when things were heaviest.

- **The Maddon touch:** Maddon didn't just coach players—he transformed them. It was like he had a magic wand, but instead of "Abracadabra," he said, "Play ball!"

  - **The Zobrist Zone:** Ben Zobrist went from bench player to super-utility star under Maddon. It was like watching a baseball Cinderella story!

  - **Arrieta's Awakening:** Jake Arrieta was struggling until Maddon got ahold of him. Suddenly, he's throwing no-hitters like they're going out of style!

  - **Bryant and Rizzo:** The "Bryzzo" combo flourished under Maddon. He turned them from promising rookies into the heart of a championship team.

- **Adapting on the fly:** Maddon wasn't a one-trick pony. He was more like a whole circus, able to change his act depending on the crowd!

  - **Tampa Bay days:** Working with a small budget? No problem! Maddon turned the Rays from bottom-dwellers to pennant winners.

- **Wrigley Field magic:** Big market, big expectations? Maddon thrived, turning the "Lovable Losers" into World Champions.

- **Angels in the outfield:** New team, new challenges? Maddon kept evolving, bringing his unique style to Anaheim.

- **More than just wins and losses:** Maddon knew that baseball was more than just a game—it was a way to make a difference.

  - **Respect 90:** Maddon's campaign to always run hard to first base wasn't just about baseball - it was about giving your all in everything you do.

  - **Hazleton Integration Project:** Back in his hometown, Maddon worked to bring together diverse communities. Home runs for social change!

  - **Thanksmas:** Every year, Maddon served meals to the needy. Because being a good manager means being a good person, too.

  - **The Maddon School of Leadership:** A leadership development program founded by Maddon, focusing on building strong, innovative leaders through community engagement, mentorship, and forward-thinking strategies.

What can we learn from Joe Maddon's wild ride? A whole lot!

- Don't be afraid to be different. Sometimes, the best ideas are the crazy ones.

- Keep things fun. When you're enjoying yourself, you play better.

- Adapt to your team. One size doesn't fit all in baseball or in life.

- Believe in your players. Sometimes, all someone needs is a chance.

Joe Maddon wasn't just a manager—he was a baseball revolutionary. He showed us that you don't have to do things the way they've always been done. You can be smart, be silly, and still be successful.

Next time you're faced with a challenge, ask yourself: "What would Maddon do?" Chances are, the answer involves thinking outside the box, keeping things fun, and believing in yourself and your team. You might not have a World Series ring (yet!), but you can definitely have Maddon's creativity and positive attitude.

In the end, Joe Maddon taught us that baseball, like life, is supposed to be fun. So go out there, try not to suck, and remember—sometimes, the best way to lead is to let your crazy flag fly!

Alright, let's dive into this like we're stepping up to the plate in the bottom of the ninth. Ready?

Lesson—Unity and Adaptability

So, you're on a baseball team, but instead of everyone working together, it's like you're all playing different sports. Chaos, right?

That's why unity and adaptability are the MVPs of team sports. They're the secret that turns a bunch of individuals into one heck of an unstoppable force.

- Unity? It's like everyone on the team is holding onto the same rope, pulling in the same direction. When you've got unity, it doesn't matter if you're the star player or warming the bench—everyone's important.

- Adaptability? That's your curveball. Life throws you surprises, and adaptability is how you hit them out of the park. It's about being flexible, rolling with the punches, and coming out swinging.

Now, Derek Jeter and Joe Maddon. These guys? They're like the Babe Ruth and Jackie Robinson of teamwork. Derek Jeter, the Yankees' captain for life, was unity personified. This guy could've let his superstar status go to his head, but nope. Jeter was all about the team. Here's how he knocked it out of the park:

- Jeter treated everyone the same, whether you were the rookie or the veteran. In the Yankees clubhouse, there were no cliques, no drama—just one united team.

- He led by example. Jeter wasn't about fancy speeches. He showed up early, stayed late, and gave 110% every single day. That kind of dedication? It's contagious.

- Jeter had this knack for making everyone feel important. He'd high-five the bat boy with the same enthusiasm as he did his fellow All-Stars. That's how you build a team that feels like family.

Now, Joe Maddon? This guy's middle name might as well be "Adaptability." As a manager, Maddon was like a baseball chameleon, always changing his approach to fit the team and the situation. Check this out:

- Maddon was famous for his wacky ideas. Pajama road trips, petting zoos in the clubhouse—you name it. Why? Because he knew that keeping things fresh and fun helped his team adapt to the grind of a long season.

- He wasn't afraid to shake things up. Maddon would put pitchers in the outfield, and have position players pitch—he kept everyone on their toes and ready for anything.

- Maddon was a master at adapting his coaching style to each player. Some guys needed a pat on the back, others needed a kick in the pants. Maddon knew exactly what buttons to push.

Time to Step Up to the Plate

So, how can you take these lessons and apply them to your own life? Glad you asked! Here are some all-star strategies to level up your teamwork and leadership game:

1. **Communication is key:** Talk to your teammates. And more importantly, listen to them. Good communication is like the oil that keeps the team engine running smoothly.

2. **Embrace your role:** Maybe you're not the cleanup hitter. That's cool. Every role on a team is important. Embrace yours and crush it.

3. **Be flexible:** Things not going according to plan? Don't freak out. Take a deep breath, adjust your approach, and keep swinging.

4. **Celebrate others' successes:** When your teammate hits a homer, cheer louder than anyone. Their win is your win.

5. **Lead by example:** Actions speak louder than words. Show up, work hard, and be the teammate you'd want to have.

6. **Keep it fun:** Remember, it's a game! When things get tense, be the one to crack a joke or start a rally dance.

7. **Stay positive:** Baseball is a game of failure. Life is too. Keep your head up and your attitude positive, no matter what.

Taking It Beyond the Diamond

Now, let's take this from the diamond to real life. Imagine you're working on a group project at school. You can use these same strategies to knock it out of the park:

- Treat everyone in your group with respect, just like Jeter did. Maybe Sarah's not great at public speaking, but she's a whiz at research. Appreciate what everyone brings to the table. Respect fuels collaboration! When team members feel valued for their contributions, they're more likely to share ideas and take risks. This inclusivity not only boosts morale but also enhances creativity, as everyone brings their strengths to the forefront, leading to richer, more epic outcomes.

- Be willing to adapt, Maddon-style. If your original idea isn't working, don't be afraid to switch gears. Maybe your history project would work better as a skit than a PowerPoint presentation. Adaptability opens doors to new possibilities. When you're willing to adjust your approach, you invite fresh perspectives that can lead to better solutions. Embracing change keeps the momentum going and ensures that your project evolves rather than stagnates. Be open to new ideas!

- Communicate clearly with your group. Set up a group chat, have regular check-ins, and make sure everyone's on the same page. Clear communication prevents misunderstandings and keeps the energy flowing. It builds trust among team members, allowing for open discussions and collaborative problem-solving. When everyone knows what's happening, they can contribute meaningfully and feel a part of the journey.

- Celebrate small victories. Finished the research phase? High fives all around! Completed the first draft? Time for a pizza party! Celebrating victories, big or small, boosts morale and keeps motivation high. It reinforces a sense of progress and accomplishment, making the group feel invested in the process. Plus, who doesn't love pizza? It's a surefire way to strengthen bonds!

- If someone's struggling, step up and help out. Remember, you're all in this together. When you support each other, you create a safety net that encourages risk-taking and vulnerability. It fosters a culture of teamwork where everyone feels comfortable seeking help and offering it. This solidarity is what transforms a group into a true team, driving everyone toward collective success.

Time for Some Self-Reflection

These skills aren't just for school, either. They'll serve you well on the little league field, in scout troops, or any time you're working with others.

Now, think about the last time you were part of a team. Maybe it was a sports team, a group project, or even just organizing a birthday party with your friends. Ask yourself:

1. How did I contribute to the team's unity?
2. Was I adaptable when things didn't go as planned?
3. Did I communicate effectively with my teammates?
4. How did I handle challenges or setbacks?
5. What could I have done better?

Remember, becoming a great team player and leader is like becoming a great ball player—it takes practice. You might strike out sometimes, but that's okay. Learn from it, adjust your swing, and step up to the plate again.

Jeter and Maddon worked at it, day in and day out. And you can too. Every time you interact with others, you have a chance to practice unity and adaptability. So next time you're working with a group, channel your inner Jeter or Maddon. Be the teammate that everyone wants to have. Because here's the thing: Life is a team sport. Whether you're on the baseball diamond, in the classroom, or out in the world, you're always part of a team. And the skills you learn from baseball—unity, adaptability, communication, leadership—these are the skills that will help you hit home runs in every area of your life.

So step up to the plate, keep your eye on the ball, and remember: In the game of life, teamwork makes the dream work!

CHAPTER 4:

Rising to the Occasion

Do you know anything about the white-knuckle world of pressure in baseball? You know that feeling when your palms get sweaty, your heart's pounding like a drum solo, and it feels like the whole world is watching?

That's pressure, and in baseball, it's as common as peanuts and Cracker Jacks.

"Pressure? That doesn't sound fun!"

But pressure is what turns coal into diamonds. It's the special sauce that makes baseball heroes. Without pressure, we wouldn't have moments that make us jump off the couch, spill our popcorn, and yell so loud the neighbors think there's a rock concert in our living room.

In baseball, pressure comes in all shapes and sizes. It could be stepping up to the plate in the bottom of the ninth, bases loaded, two outs, your team down by three. Or maybe it's pitching in Game 7 of the World Series, knowing that one bad throw could cost your team everything. Heck, it could even be trying to break a record that's older than your grandpa's lucky socks. Every single baseball star you've ever heard of, from Babe Ruth to Mike Trout, has faced pressure that would make most of us curl up in a ball and cry for our mommies. The difference? These guys don't just handle pressure—they eat it for breakfast and ask for seconds!

Learning how these baseball heroes deal with pressure isn't just about becoming a better player. It's about becoming a better you. Because let's face it, life throws us curveballs all the time. Maybe it's a big test at school, or trying out for the school play, or asking your crush to the dance. The skills you learn from baseball's pressure cookers can help you knock life's challenges out of the park. Now, don't get me wrong. Pressure in baseball isn't some rare beast that only shows up once in a blue moon. Nope, it's as much a part of the game as hot dogs and the seventh-inning stretch. Every single game has moments where the pressure's cranked up to 11. And how a player handles these moments? Well, that can be the difference between being a hero or a zero, between champagne showers in the locker room or a long, quiet bus ride home.

But here's the cool bit: dealing with pressure isn't some magical talent that you're born with. It's a skill, just like hitting a curveball or fielding a grounder. And like any skill, you can practice it, improve it, and master it. The baseball stars we're gonna talk about? They've turned handling pressure into an art form.

Speaking of which, let me introduce you to the stars of our show today. First up, we've got Reggie Jackson. This guy was so clutch in big moments that they called him "Mr. October." October, for those of you who might be new to baseball, is when the World Series happens. It's like the Super Bowl, but way cooler and spread out over a week. Then we've got the 2004 Boston Red Sox. Now, these guys didn't just handle pressure - they laughed in its face, gave it a wedgie, and sent it home crying to its mama. They pulled off something so incredible, so unbelievable, that if it were a movie, you'd roll your eyes and say, "Yeah, right. Like that could ever happen."

Reggie Jackson's story is all about how one guy can rise to the occasion when it matters most. The Red Sox? They're gonna show us how a whole team can band together when the odds are stacked against them higher than a triple-decker sandwich. These stories aren't just about baseball. They're about guts, glory, and the kind of never-say-die attitude that turns ordinary players into legends. They're about looking pressure dead in the eye and saying, "You don't scare me. I've got this."

Ready to play ball? Let's do this!

Reggie Jackson—Mr. October's Moment

Once upon a time, there was a guy who was cooler under pressure than a polar bear wearing sunglasses. I'm talking about Reggie Jackson, the man, the myth, the legend they called "Mr. October."

Now, why "Mr. October"? Was it because he really liked pumpkin spice lattes? Nope! It was because when the leaves started turning and the World Series rolled around, Reggie turned into a baseball-crushing machine. This guy didn't just handle pressure—he ate it for breakfast, lunch, and dinner, and then asked for seconds—and thirds.

It's 1977, Game 6 of the World Series. The New York Yankees versus the Los Angeles Dodgers. The Yankees are up 3 games to 2, but the Dodgers aren't going down without a fight. The whole season comes down to this. Reggie steps up to the plate, and BANG! He smacks a home run. The crowd goes wild! But Reggie? He's just getting started.

His next at-bat? CRACK! Another home run! The stadium is shaking! People are losing their minds! But our man Reggie? Just too cool.

Then comes his third at-bat. The pressure's so thick you could cut it with a knife. Everyone's thinking, "There's no way he does it again, right?" WRONG! Reggie swings, and POW! A third home run! The crowd is going bananas! Reggie's just hit three home runs in a row, on three consecutive pitches, in a World Series game. It's like he's playing a video game and someone gave him all the cheat codes!

This, champs, is what we call "rising to the occasion." When the lights were brightest, when the pressure was highest when everyone was watching, Reggie Jackson didn't just perform—he put on a show for the ages.

But the million-dollar question: How did he do it? How did Reggie stay so cool when the heat was on?

Well, Mr. October's about to give us a masterclass in handling pressure.

- First off, Reggie had confidence coming out of his ears. He once said, "I don't exactly know what it means to be a superstar, but I guess I am one." Talk about swagger! But here's the thing—this wasn't just empty bragging. Reggie backed it up with hard work. He prepared like a madman, practicing his swing over and over and over again. By the time the big moment came, he'd already played it out in his head a thousand times.

- Reggie also had a secret weapon: he loved the pressure. While other players might've been shaking in their cleats, Reggie was like a kid on Christmas morning. He lived for these moments. The bigger the game, the brighter the lights, the more Reggie wanted to be there. He once said, "I was born to play in front of 50,000 people. I wasn't born to pitch in front of 50 people." Talk about embracing the spotlight!

- But don't think for a second that Reggie didn't feel the pressure. Oh, he felt it alright. The difference was, he used it. Instead of letting the butterflies in his stomach throw him off his game, he channeled that nervous energy into his performance. It was like he turned the pressure into rocket fuel for his bat!

- Reggie also had a knack for blocking out distractions. In the batter's box, with 50,000 screaming fans and millions watching on TV, Reggie had a laser focus. In his mind, it was just him, the pitcher, and the ball. Everything else faded away. It's like he had his own personal bubble of calm in the middle of a hurricane.

- And here's another trick up Reggie's sleeve: he kept things simple. In high-pressure moments, it's easy to overthink, to get lost in the "what-ifs." But not Reggie. His approach? See ball, hit ball. He didn't try to do too much or be a hero. He just focused on doing what he knew he could do.

- But perhaps the biggest lesson we can learn from Reggie is this: he wasn't afraid to fail. Sounds weird, right? But think about it—when you're so scared of messing up, you get tense, you play it safe, you don't swing for the fences. Reggie? He knew strikeouts were part of the game. He was willing to risk failure for the chance at greatness. And more often than not, he achieved that greatness.

So, whether it's a big game, a tough test, or any high-pressure situation, channel your inner Reggie Jackson. Work hard to prepare, love the challenge, focus on what you can control, keep it simple, and don't be afraid to swing for the fences.

Remember, pressure can burst pipes, but it can also create diamonds. Reggie Jackson chose to be a diamond. And in those shining October moments, with the whole world watching, boy did he sparkle.

2004 Boston Red Sox—Reversing the Curse

Baseball fans! We're about to dive into a story so epic, so unbelievable, that if it were a movie, you'd roll your eyes and say, "Yeah, right. Like that could ever happen."

But guess what? It did happen. And it's all about the 2004 Boston Red Sox.

It's October 2004. The Red Sox are playing their arch-nemesis, the New York Yankees, in the American League Championship Series (ALCS). The winner goes to the World Series. The loser goes home to cry into their cornflakes. And let me tell you, the Red Sox had done a lot of cornflake-crying over the years.

See, the Red Sox hadn't won a World Series since 1918. That's 86 years of heartbreak, folks. People called it "The Curse of the Bambino," all because they sold Babe Ruth to the Yankees way back when. Talk about a bad trade! So here they are, facing the Yankees, and things are looking bleaker than a rainy day at Fenway Park. The Red Sox are down 3 games to 0 in a best-of-seven series. In the history of baseball, no team had ever come back from a 3-0 deficit in the playoffs. Ever. It was like being down 20-0 in the bottom of the ninth with two outs. Impossible, right?

But here's where it gets good. The Red Sox? They didn't get the memo that they were supposed to roll over and play dead. Nope. They looked at that 3-0 deficit and said, "Hold my Gatorade."

- Game 4 rolls around. The Yankees are up 4-3 in the 9th inning. The Red Sox are three outs away from another year of misery. But then, like a superhero swooping in to save the day, up steps David Ortiz, aka "Big Papi." CRACK! He hits

71

a walk-off home run in extra innings. Red Sox win 6-4. The comeback has begun!

- Game 5, and it's déjà vu all over again. Extra innings, Ortiz at the plate. BAM! A single drives in the winning run. Red Sox win 5-4. The Yankees are sweating now.

- Game 6 is where things get really wild. Curt Schilling, the Red Sox pitcher, takes the mound with an injured ankle so bad he's literally bleeding into his sock. But does he back down? No sir! He pitches like a man possessed, leading the Red Sox to a 4-2 victory. The blood-stained sock becomes the stuff of legend.

- And then comes Game 7. Winner takes all. The pressure's so thick you could cut it with a knife. But the Red Sox? They're in the zone. They crush the Yankees 10-3, completing the greatest comeback in baseball history.

- But wait, there's more! The Red Sox ride this wave of momentum all the way to a World Series sweep against the St. Louis Cardinals. The curse is broken! 86 years of heartbreak? Gone faster than you can say "Reverse the curse!"

So how did they do it? How did the Red Sox pull off the impossible?

It wasn't just skill (though they had plenty of that). It was mental toughness that would make a Navy SEAL say, "Whoa, those guys are tough!"

- First off, they never stopped believing. Even when everyone else had written them off, the Red Sox kept the faith. They took it one game at a time, one inning at a time, one pitch at a time. They didn't get overwhelmed by the big picture. They just focused on what was right in front of them.

- Then there was the teamwork. This wasn't a one-man show. Sure, Ortiz and Schilling had their hero moments, but every player stepped up when it counted. They had each other's backs. When one guy faltered, another picked him up. It was like they were all pulling on the same rope, and that rope was tied to a truck stuck in the mud of an 86-year losing streak.

- And let's talk about resilience. These guys bounced back from setbacks like they were made of rubber. Bad call by the ump? Shake it off. Error in the field? Make up for it next play. Down 3-0 in the series? Just means we've got them right where we want 'em!

- The Red Sox also mastered the art of staying loose under pressure. They called themselves "The Idiots," not because they were dumb, but because they refused to get caught up in the pressure and history. They cracked jokes, grew crazy caveman beards, and played like they had nothing to lose. And you know what? It worked!

But perhaps the biggest lesson from the 2004 Red Sox is this: never, ever give up. When the odds are stacked against you, when everyone's counting you out, that's when you dig deep and find out what you're really made of.

Next time you're facing your own 3-0 deficit, whether it's a tough test, a big game, or any challenge that seems impossible, remember the 2004 Red Sox. Believe in yourself. Trust your teammates. Stay resilient. Keep it loose.

And, never, ever give up. Because sometimes, the greatest victories come when defeat seems certain. And those victories? They're the ones you'll remember forever.

Lesson—Mental Toughness and Belief

Huddle right up! We've just seen two incredible examples of mental toughness and belief in action. But what exactly are these super skills, and how can you develop them?

Don't worry, we're about to break it down faster than a speedster stealing second base.

- First off, let's talk mental toughness. It's not about having muscles in your brain (though that would be pretty cool). Mental toughness is like having a forcefield around your mind that keeps out doubt, fear, and negativity. It's the ability to stay focused and perform at your best, even when the pressure's cranked up to eleven.

- Belief, on the other hand, is like your mind's cheerleader. It's that little voice in your head that says, "You've got this!" even when things look bleaker than a Chicago Cubs fan's mood before 2016. Belief is what keeps you swinging for the fences when everyone else is bunting.

Now, Reggie Jackson and the 2004 Red Sox? They had mental toughness and belief coming out of their ears. Reggie stepped up to the plate in the World Series like he was playing a friendly game of backyard baseball. The Red Sox looked at a 3-0 deficit and said, "Challenge accepted!" That's mental toughness and belief in action, folks.

Your Turn to Level Up

"How can I develop these superpowers for myself?"

Grab your mental batting gloves, because we're about to hit you with some strategies that'll have you handling pressure like a pro:

1. **Practice under pressure:** Ever heard the saying "practice makes perfect"? Well, for handling pressure, it's more like "practice under pressure makes perfect under pressure." Set up mock high-pressure situations. Want to nail that performance? Set up intense mock scenarios. Athletes? Crank up the crowd noise. Test-takers? Do your practice with a ticking clock breathing down your neck. You're training to thrive, not just survive.

2. **Visualize success:** Close your eyes and imagine yourself succeeding in high-pressure situations. See yourself hitting that game-winning homer or acing that tough test. Here's the thing: your brain? It's not the sharpest when it comes to separating reality from what you imagine. Seriously. Whether you're daydreaming about your victory lap or actually running it, your brain responds the same way. Every time you mentally rehearse success, those neurons light up like it's already happening. You're literally rewiring your brain to believe you've been there, done that. So, when the real deal hits? Your brain thinks, "Oh, we got this!" You've already practiced winning in your mind, so that sense of unstoppable awesomeness is primed and ready to roll. Think of it as your mental dress rehearsal for greatness.

3. **Control your breathing:** When the pressure's on, our breathing often goes haywire. Practice deep, slow breaths.

It's like hitting the "calm down" button for your body and mind. You can use this trick anytime you're feeling the pressure:

a. First, sit or stand up straight.

b. Now, take a big, slow breath through your nose—imagine you're sniffing a delicious pizza. Fill your belly like a balloon.

c. Hold it for a second.

d. Then, slowly exhale through your mouth, like you're blowing out birthday candles—nice and easy.

e. See? Just like that, you've hit the "calm down" button. No more nervous squirrel.

4. **Focus on what you can control:** You can't control the weather, the umpire's calls, or what other people do. Stressing over those things? Waste. Of. Energy. So, focus on what you can control. And, what can you control?

a. *Your effort:* show up, give your best, and leave it all on the field, court, or test paper.

b. *Your attitude:* choose positivity and resilience, even when things get tough.

c. *And your preparation:* practice, study, and put in the work beforehand.

5. Focus on those things, and let the rest roll off your back like water off a duck. You'll feel more confident, and that's when the magic happens.

6. **Develop a routine:** Having a set routine can be like a security blanket for your mind, or like your lucky socks. It gives you something familiar to focus on when everything else feels chaotic. It could be warming up the same way, listening to your favorite song, or even just taking a few deep breaths. It's your brain's way of saying, "Hey, I've got this!" When things around you are chaotic, your routine is like a safety net that keeps you focused and calm.

7. **Positive self-talk:** Be your own biggest cheerleader. Instead of thinking, "What if I mess up?", imagine you're about to hit the winning shot—are you telling yourself you'll miss? No way! You're telling yourself you're going to nail it. Start saying, "I'm ready," "I've practiced," or "I'm going to crush this." The more you pump yourself up, the more your brain believes it!

8. **Learn from setbacks:** Everyone strikes out sometimes. But here's the trick: don't see it as a failure, see it as a lesson. Ask yourself, "What could I do differently next time?" Everyone strikes out once in a while—even the pros. The key is to treat setbacks as learning opportunities, not failures, and to bounce back stronger than before.

9. **Stay in the moment:** Don't get ahead of yourself. If you're playing a game, think about making that next pass, not winning the whole thing. If you're taking a test, think about the question in front of you, not your final grade. The best way to do well is to focus on what's right in front of you— not what comes next! Keep it simple, one moment at a time. It just makes total sense because it's impossible to live in the

past or the future. Live in the present moment, because that is the only time you can take action for a better tomorrow.

Taking It Beyond the Diamond

Now, let's take these strategies and apply them to real-life situations you might face:

- Got a big test coming up? Use visualization to see yourself calmly answering questions. Develop a pre-test routine, like listening to a specific song or doing some light stretches. During the test, focus on one question at a time instead of worrying about your overall score.

- Playing in a championship game? Practice your breathing exercises during timeouts. Use positive self-talk to pump yourself up. "I've practiced for this. I'm ready." Focus on playing your best, not on winning or losing.

- Nervous about a public speaking gig? Visualize yourself delivering your speech confidently. Practice your speech under pressure by recording yourself or speaking in front of friends. Develop a pre-speech routine to calm your nerves.

- Stepping into unfamiliar territory can feel daunting, like facing a legendary pitcher for the first time. Instead of shying away, embrace it! Adapt your mindset by recognizing that every expert was once a beginner. Starting a new hobby? Whether it's coding, painting, or playing an instrument, visualize yourself mastering it step by step. Picture the progress you'll make over time, celebrating each small win.

- When life throws a curveball—like a job application rejection—don't let it be a strikeout. Instead, reframe it as a valuable lesson! Mental toughness means understanding that setbacks are just setups for comebacks.

Mental toughness and belief are like muscles—the more you use them, the stronger they get. So start small. Maybe it's staying calm during a pop quiz or not freaking out when you're up to bat with two outs. Every time you face a challenge and come out the other side, you're building your mental toughness and belief.

Time for Some Self-Reflection

And here's a pro tip: Reflect on your experiences. After a high-pressure situation, ask yourself:

1. What went well?
2. What could I have done better?
3. How did I handle the pressure?
4. What can I learn from this for next time?

Reflection is important because it helps you learn and grow, turning every experience—good or bad—into a stepping stone for improvement.

Lastly, remember this: Pressure is a privilege. It means you're doing something important, something that matters. So next time you feel those butterflies in your stomach, smile. It means you're about to do something awesome.

So there you have it. Mental toughness and belief: the secret weapons of sports legends and straight-A students alike.

They turned Reggie Jackson into Mr. October and helped the Red Sox reverse an 86-year-old curse. They undoubtedly can help you knock your challenges out of the park too.

CHAPTER 5:

Learning From Strike Outs

Alrighty, let's talk about something that happens to every baseball player, from the sandlot to the big leagues. Something that can make your stomach drop faster than a knuckleball and your confidence shrink like a jersey in the hot wash.

That's right, we're talking about failure.

"Failure? That doesn't sound like much fun!"

And you're right, it's not. Failure in baseball can feel like you've got a glove full of rocks and cleats made of lead. It's striking out with the bases loaded in the bottom of the ninth. It's watching a fly ball sail over your head as the winning run scores. It's finishing dead last in the standings when you thought you had a shot at the pennant. But here's the curveball: failure, as much as it stinks, is actually one of the best teachers you'll ever have. It's like the tough-love coach of life, showing you exactly where you need to improve. And in baseball? Failure is as common as peanuts and Cracker Jacks.

Think about it. Even the best hitters in the game fail way more often than they succeed. A .300 batting average is considered excellent, but that means the batter's failing 7 out of 10 times! Can you imagine if you only got 30% of the questions right on a test and your teacher said, "Great job, champ!"?

But here's the secret: it's not about how often you fail. It's about what you do after you fail. Do you throw your bat and sulk back to the dugout? Or do you take a deep breath, think about what went wrong, and figure out how to do better next time?

The baseball stars we're gonna talk about? They're not just great because they hit a ton of home runs or threw a bunch of no-hitters. They're great because they knew how to bounce back when things went wrong. They turned their strikeouts into learning opportunities, and their errors into motivation to improve. And let me tell you, if you can learn this skill - turning failure into fuel for success—you'll be unstoppable. Not just in baseball, but in everything you do. School giving you a hard time? Use that tough test to figure out what you need to study more. Didn't make the team you wanted? Use that as motivation to practice harder and come back stronger next year.

Now, don't get me wrong. Failure isn't fun. It's not like broccoli, where your parents say "It's good for you!" and you suddenly start loving it. Failure hurts. It can make you want to quit, to give up, to say "I'm just not good enough." But that's where the magic happens. Because it's in those moments, when you're down in the dirt with skinned knees and a bruised ego, that you have a choice. You can stay down, or you can get back up, dust yourself off, and try again. And every time you choose to get back up? You're getting stronger, smarter, better.

In baseball, like in life, failure isn't the opposite of success. It's part of success. It's the gritty, tough, character-building part that nobody likes to talk about. But it's the part that separates the good from the great, the ones who give up from the ones who go down in history.

Speaking of going down in history, let me introduce you to the all-stars of our failure-to-success story. First up, we've got the Sultan of Swat himself, Babe Ruth. Now, you might know Babe as the guy who hit more home runs than anybody thought possible. But did you know he started out as a pitcher? And not just any pitcher—a darn good one! We're gonna dive into how Babe turned the "failure" of his pitching career into the launch pad for becoming the greatest slugger the game had ever seen.

Then we've got the Chicago Cubs. Now, if you want to talk about a team that knows failure, the Cubs wrote the book. These guys went 108 years without winning a World Series. That's longer than most people live! But in 2016, they finally broke the curse. We're gonna look at how a century of setbacks set the stage for one of the most dramatic comebacks in sports history.

These stories aren't just about baseball. They're about grit, perseverance, and the kind of never-say-die attitude that turns strikeouts into home runs and curses into championships. They're about looking failure in the eye and saying, "Nice try, but I'm not done yet."

Let's do roll!

Babe Ruth—From Mound to Moonshots

Step right into the batter's box and make yourself ready to take a swing at one of the greatest stories in baseball history. We're talking about a guy who didn't just play the game—he changed it forever.

Ladies, gentlemen, and sluggers, put your hands together for the one, the only, Babe Ruth!

Now, when you hear "Babe Ruth," what comes to mind? Home runs, right? The Bambino swinging for the fences, pointing to the stands, calling his shot. But here's a curveball for you: Babe Ruth started his career as a pitcher. And not just any pitcher—he was ace material!

- It's 1914, and 19-year-old George Herman "Babe" Ruth Jr. steps onto the mound for the Boston Red Sox. He's a southpaw with a wicked fastball and a curve that falls off the table. In his first full season, he goes 18-8 with a 2.44 ERA. That's not just good - that's "Hey, this kid might be something special" good.

- For the next few years, Ruth dominates on the mound. In 1916, he leads the league with a 1.75 ERA. In 1917, he throws 35 complete games. That's not a typo—35 complete games! Nowadays, pitchers get a standing ovation if they make it through seven innings.

- But here's where our story takes a twist. See, Ruth wasn't just good at throwing the ball—he could hit it a country mile too. And the Red Sox, being smarter than the average bear, thought, "Hey, why should this guy only play every four or five days when he could be crushing baseballs every day?"

So, little by little, Ruth starts playing the outfield when he's not pitching. And boy, does he make an impact! In 1918, he leads the league in home runs... with 11. Yeah, 11. Back then, that was a lot. Baseball was more about bunts and stolen bases. Home runs were like finding a four-leaf clover - rare and exciting. But Ruth? He's not content with 11. In 1919, he hits 29 homers, shattering the previous single-season record. The baseball world is flipping its collective lid. It's like someone showed up to a horse race riding a motorcycle.

Here's where we get to the "failure" part of our story. Because from one perspective, Ruth's pitching career was coming to an end. He goes from being one of the best pitchers in the league to barely taking the mound at all. If you were just looking at his pitching stats, you'd think, "Man, this guy's career really took a nosedive."

But he doesn't see it as a failure. He sees it as an opportunity. An opportunity to reinvent himself, to become something the baseball world has never seen before.

- In 1920, Ruth is traded to the New York Yankees. And that's when things get really wild. In his first year with the Yankees, Ruth hits 54 home runs. Fifty-four! That's more than any other American League team hit that year. Not player—team.

- Ruth doesn't just hit home runs—he obliterates them. He hits them farther than anyone thought possible. People start calling his home runs "Ruthian blasts" because there's no other way to describe them. He's not just playing baseball - he's revolutionizing it.

- By the time he hangs up his cleats, Ruth has hit 714 home runs. He's turned the home run from a rarity into the most exciting play in baseball. He's become the face of the sport, a larger-than-life figure who transcends the game.

So, what can we learn from the Babe's journey from the mound to moonshots?

- **Be open to change:** Ruth could have stubbornly stuck to pitching. Instead, he embraced a new role and became a legend.

- **Use your strengths:** Ruth was a good pitcher, but he was an otherworldly hitter. He played to his strengths and changed the game.

- **Don't let others define your success:** To some, giving up pitching might have looked like failure. Ruth turned it into the launch pad for unprecedented success.

- **Keep improving:** Ruth didn't just become a good hitter—he became the best hitter. He constantly pushed himself to improve.

- **Have fun:** Through it all, Ruth played with joy. He loved the game, and it showed in how he played.

Sometimes, what looks like failure is just a detour on the road to greatness. It's about being willing to reinvent yourself, to try new things, to swing for the fences even when everyone else is playing small ball.

So next time you face a setback, whether it's in baseball or in life, remember Babe Ruth. Remember that the end of one thing can be the beginning of something even greater.

Now, get swinging for the fences!

Chicago Cubs—A Century in the Making

Are you ready for a story that's part tragedy, part comedy, and all heart. We're talking about the Chicago Cubs and their 108-year journey from lovable losers to World Series champions.

This isn't just a baseball story—it's an epic saga that would make Homer scratch his head and say, "Whoa, that's a long time!"

Let's paint the picture: It's 1908, and the Chicago Cubs have just won the World Series. Life is good on the North Side of Chicago. Little do they know, they've just bought a ticket for a roller coaster ride that'll last longer than anyone could have imagined.

- Fast forward through World War I, the Great Depression, World War II, the Cold War, the Moon landing, disco, and the invention of the internet—the Cubs still haven't won another World Series. They've become the "lovable losers," the team that breaks your heart so often you start to think it's just part of being a fan.

- But it's not like they weren't trying. Oh boy, were they trying. They made it to the World Series in 1910, 1918, 1929, 1932, 1935, 1938, and 1945. Each time, they came up short. It's like they were allergic to championship trophies!

- Then there's 1969. The Cubs are in first place, looking like they might finally break the curse. But faster than you can say "black cat" (which, by the way, actually ran across the field during a crucial game), they collapse. The "Miracle Mets" zoom past them, and Cubs fans are left wondering if they'll ever see a championship.

- How about 1984? The Cubs are one win away from the World Series. They've got their ace on the mound. It's in the bag, right? Nope! They lose three straight games and watch the Padres go to the World Series instead.

- Then there's 2003. Oh boy, 2003. The Cubs are five outs away from the World Series. Five! But then... well, let's just say a foul ball, a fan, and a complete meltdown happened. Cubs lose, and the drought continues.

- At this point, you'd forgive Cubs fans for throwing in the towel. But here's the thing about Cubs fans—they don't quit. They're like the Black Knight from Monty Python, getting their arms and legs chopped off but still saying, "It's just a flesh wound!"

- But then, something starts to change. In 2009, the Ricketts family buys the team. They bring in Theo Epstein as president of baseball operations in 2011. This is the guy who helped the Red Sox break their own curse in 2004. Suddenly, there's a plan. A real, honest-to-goodness plan to build a winner.

- The Cubs start rebuilding from the ground up. They draft smart. They trade smart. They sign smart free agents. They invest in analytics and player development. It's like they've gone from playing checkers to playing 3D chess.

- Young stars start emerging. Kris Bryant, Anthony Rizzo, Javier Báez—these guys aren't just talented, they're fearless. They don't know about curses or billy goats or black cats. They just want to win.

- In 2015, the Cubs make it to the National League Championship Series. They get swept, but hey, progress! Cubs fans start to think, "Maybe, just maybe..."

And then comes 2016. The Cubs win 103 games in the regular season. They storm through the playoffs. They make it to the World Series, facing off against another team with a long championship drought—the Cleveland Indians.

The World Series is a nail-biter. The Cubs fall behind 3 games to 1. It's looking like another heartbreak. But these Cubs? They're different. They win Game 5. They win Game 6. It all comes down to Game 7. Game 7 is like a microcosm of the Cubs' entire history. They take a lead. They lose the lead. There's rain. There's extra innings. It's joy, heartbreak, and heart attacks all rolled into one.

And then... it happens. At 12:47 AM on November 3, 2016, Kris Bryant fields a ground ball, throws to Anthony Rizzo, and... the Cubs win the World Series! 108 years of waiting, over in an instant. The city of Chicago erupts. Fans are crying, laughing, hugging strangers. It's like every Christmas, birthday, and Fourth of July rolled into one.

The Cubs aren't losers anymore—they're champions!

So what can we learn from the Cubs' century-long journey?

- **Never give up:** 108 years is a long time to wait for anything. But Cubs fans kept believing, year after year.

- **Build a strong foundation:** The Cubs' success didn't happen overnight. It took years of smart planning and development.

- **Learn from failure:** Each heartbreak taught the Cubs something. They used those lessons to get better.

- **Believe in yourself:** When the Cubs were down 3-1 in the World Series, they didn't panic. They believed they could come back—and they did.

- **Enjoy the journey:** As tough as the losing was, being a Cubs fan was about more than winning. It was about community, tradition, and love of the game.

No drought lasts forever, no curse is unbreakable. It's about keeping faith, working hard, and being ready when your moment finally comes.

When you're facing a long odds or a seemingly impossible task, remember the Chicago Cubs. Remember that sometimes, the sweetest victories are the ones that take the longest to achieve.

Lesson—Adaptability and Persistence

Alright, team, huddle up! We've just witnessed two incredible stories of triumph over adversity. Babe Ruth turning a "failed" pitching career into legendary slugging status, and the Chicago Cubs transforming a century of heartbreak into World Series glory.

But what's the epic secret here? What turned these potential strikeouts into home runs? Two words, folks: adaptability and persistence.

Now, let's break these down faster than a speedster stealing second base.

- Adaptability is like being a Swiss Army knife in cleats. It's the ability to change your game plan when curveballs come your way. In baseball, and in life, things rarely go exactly as planned. Adaptability is what lets you swing for the fences even when the pitch isn't what you expected.

- Persistence, on the other hand, is like being a human boomerang. No matter how many times life knocks you down, you keep coming back. It's the grit to keep swinging even when you're in a slump, the determination to keep showing up to practice even when you're riding the bench.

Babe Ruth and the Chicago Cubs? They had adaptability and persistence coming out of their caps. Ruth adapted from being a star pitcher to a legendary slugger, persisting through the challenge of learning a new position. The Cubs adapted their entire organization, persisting through 108 years of disappointment to finally clinch that elusive championship.

But how can you develop these superpowers for yourself?

Your Time to Shine

Well, we're about to hit you with some strategies that'll have you adapting and persisting like a pro:

1. **Embrace change:** Don't fear it, welcome it! Change is your opportunity to grow. Next time something unexpected happens, instead of panicking, ask yourself, "How can I use this to my advantage?"

   a. **Example:** Think of players like Derek Jeter, who faced massive changes in the game, from shifting positions to adapting to new teammates. When change hits, try reframing your perspective. Instead of seeing obstacles, view them as chances to develop new skills. Ask, "What new strengths can I cultivate from this situation?"

b. **Strategy:** Keep a "Change Journal." Whenever change happens, jot down what you can learn from it and how you can pivot. Over time, you'll see a treasure trove of growth opportunities!

1. **Be flexible in your thinking:** There's usually more than one way to solve a problem. If your first approach doesn't work, brainstorm alternatives. Remember, Babe Ruth didn't just give up when his pitching career ended—he found a new way to contribute.

   a. **Example:** Picture the Chicago Cubs in 2016, adjusting their game plans and strategies throughout the season to finally break the curse. They faced challenges head-on and adapted their strategies to rise to the occasion.

   b. **Strategy:** Practice brainstorming sessions. Gather your team (or friends) and throw out all kinds of solutions, no matter how outlandish. You never know which wild idea could turn into a winning game plan!

2. **Learn continuously:** The more skills and knowledge you have, the more adaptable you'll be. Read books, try new hobbies, and learn from others. You never know when that random fact or skill might come in handy!

   a. **Example:** Take a cue from legendary coach Tony La Russa, who constantly evolved his strategies by studying different approaches to the game.

   b. **Strategy:** Set a personal challenge to learn something new every month—whether it's a skill, a sport, or even a random fact. You might stumble upon something that becomes your new secret weapon on and off the field!

3. **Set goals, but be flexible about how you achieve them:** The Cubs' goal was always to win the World Series, but they had to change their approach many times over the years.

   a. **Example:** They faced numerous setbacks but remained committed to their goal while allowing flexibility in their methods.

   b. **Strategy:** Create a vision board for your goals, but leave space for adjustments. If a path doesn't work, don't erase it—cross it out and draw a new route!

4. **Develop a growth mindset:** Believe that you can improve and grow. Challenges aren't threats—they're opportunities to learn and get better.

   a. **Example:** Michael Jordan was cut from his high school basketball team. Instead of giving up, he saw it as a chance to work harder, and look where that got him!

   b. **Strategy:** When facing a setback, ask yourself, "What can I learn from this?" Keep a "Growth Log" where you document your challenges and the lessons learned. Over time, you'll build a roadmap of resilience!

5. **Practice resilience:** When you face a setback, acknowledge your feelings, but don't dwell on them. Ask yourself, "What can I learn from this? How can I do better next time?"

   a. **Example:** When a player strikes out, the best ones shake it off, learn from it, and focus on the next at-bat.

b. **Strategy:** After a setback, take a moment to reflect, but then set a timer for 10 minutes to wallow. Once it's up, shift gears! Write down what you learned and how you'll tackle the next challenge.

6. **Celebrate small victories:** Persistence is easier when you acknowledge your progress. Did you improve your batting average this season? Celebrate it, even if you didn't win the championship.

   a. **Example:** After the Cubs won the National League pennant in 2016, they celebrated each step leading to the World Series—because every win matters!

   b. **Strategy:** Create a "Victory Jar." Every time you achieve something, big or small, write it down and toss it in. On tough days, pull a few out to remind yourself of your progress!

7. **Find your motivation:** What drives you? Is it personal growth? Proving doubters wrong? Making your family proud? Find your "why" and let it fuel your persistence.

   a. **Example:** Think of athletes who play not just for themselves but for their families and communities. That emotional connection is a powerful motivator.

   b. **Strategy:** Write a personal mission statement. Pin it where you can see it daily. Let that be your guiding star whenever the going gets tough!

Taking It Beyond the Diamond

Now, let's take these strategies and apply them to real-life situations you might face:

- Struggling in math class? Adapt your study methods. If reading the textbook isn't working, try watching video tutorials or working with a study group. Persist by tackling a few problems each day, even when it's tough.

- Didn't make the starting lineup? Adapt by focusing on improving specific skills the coach mentioned. Persist by giving 100% in practice and staying ready for your opportunity.

- Facing a tough project at school? Adapt by breaking it into smaller, manageable tasks. Persist by working on it consistently, even when you'd rather be doing something else.

- Life can throw a busy schedule your way, like a wild pitch that comes out of nowhere. Instead of feeling overwhelmed, adapt by prioritizing your tasks. Use tools like calendars or apps to break your day into manageable chunks.

- Criticism can sting, but instead of letting it knock you down like a bad call, adapt by viewing it as constructive feedback. Embrace it as a chance to grow, like a player who studies game footage to improve performance.

Adaptability and persistence are like muscles—the more you use them, the stronger they get. So start small. Maybe it's trying a new approach to solving a problem, or sticking with a challenging task for just five minutes longer than you usually would.

Every time you adapt to a new situation or persist through a challenge, you're building these crucial skills.

Time for Some Self-Reflection

And here's a pro tip: Always, always reflect on your experiences. After facing a challenge, ask yourself:

1. How did I adapt to this situation?
2. Where did I show persistence?
3. What did I learn that I can use next time?

This reflection helps you recognize your growth and learn from every experience, turning each challenge into a stepping stone for improvement.

Lastly, remember this: Adaptability and persistence aren't about never failing. They're about learning, growing, and keeping going despite the failures. Babe Ruth struck out 1,330 times in his career. The Cubs lost thousands of games during their 108-year drought. But they kept adapting, kept persisting, and eventually, they made history.

Adaptability and persistence: they turned Babe Ruth from a pitcher into the Sultan of Swat and helped the Cubs go from lovable losers to World Series champs. And with practice, they can help you knock your challenges out of the park too.

Remember, every strikeout is just practice for your next home run!

Surprise!

You've just earned your VIP Clubhouse Pass! Want to know what baseball superstars really eat before the big game? Curious about their secret pre-game fuel routines? Scan this QR code to join the pros in the clubhouse!

CHAPTER 6:

Game Changers

Game Changers isn't just about baseball—it's about shaking things up, turning the world on its head, and showing everyone what's possible when you dare to be different.

It's a crisp spring day, the smell of fresh-cut grass in the air. The ballpark's buzzing with excitement. But hold up—something's different. There's tension in the air, like static electricity before a storm. Why? Because today, someone's about to do something that's never been done before. They're about to change the game.

That's what this chapter's all about—the rebels, the dreamers, the ones who looked at the rules and said, "Nah, I think I'll write my own playbook." We're talking about the barrier breakers, the folks who didn't just push the envelope—they tore it up and used the pieces to make a paper airplane. Now, breaking barriers in baseball? It's not just about the sport. It's like dropping a pebble in a pond—the ripples spread out, touching everything. When someone changes the game on the diamond, they're often changing the game of life for a whole lot of people.

So why should you care? Well, champs, here's the deal: understanding how these brave souls changed baseball might just light a fire under you. Maybe you'll look at that thing everyone says you can't do and think, "Watch me." But let's get real for a second. Breaking barriers? It's not all home runs and high-fives. It's more like trying to hit a 100 mph fastball while the pitcher's also throwing insults your way.

- Skepticism? Check.

- Criticism? You bet.

- Discrimination? Unfortunately, yeah.

It takes guts, determination, and the kind of toughness you can't learn from a playbook. When you break through, you're not just winning for yourself. You're clearing the path for everyone coming up behind you. You're changing minds, opening doors, and showing the world what's possible.

In this chapter, we're gonna meet two all-stars of barrier-breaking:

- **Hank Aaron:** The guy who swung his way past Babe Ruth's home run record—and a whole lot of hatred.

- **Kim Ng:** The woman who slide-tackled the glass ceiling in baseball's front office.

These two didn't just play the game—they changed it. And their stories? They're not just about baseball. They're about showing the world that the only limits that matter are the ones you put on yourself.

So, ready to meet our first game-changer? Let's talk about Hammerin' Hank Aaron.

Hank Aaron—Hammering Through Hatred

It's April 8, 1974. The Atlanta Braves are playing the L.A. Dodgers. Up to bat steps a man with the weight of history—and a whole lot of hate—on his shoulders.

This is Hank Aaron, and he's about to do something huge.

CRACK! The ball soars over the left-field fence. Home run number 715. Babe Ruth's record is toast, and Aaron rounds the bases into history. But hold up. Let's rewind a bit. Because getting to this moment? It wasn't just a walk in the park. It was more like running a marathon. Through a minefield. In cleats.

- **The quest:** Aaron wasn't just chasing a number. He was chasing the ghost of Babe Ruth, the larger-than-life legend of baseball. And not everyone was cheering him on.

- **The ugly truth:** As Aaron got closer to the record, the hate mail started pouring in. We're talking death threats, folks. Vile, racist garbage that would make your stomach turn.

- **The pressure cooker:** Imagine trying to focus on hitting a tiny ball with a stick while knowing there are people out there who want to hurt you just for being good at your job. That's what Aaron was dealing with. Every. Single. Day.

But here's where it gets good. Aaron? He didn't crack. He didn't quit. He stood tall, kept his cool, and let his bat do the talking.

- **Mental toughness 101:** Aaron once said, "My motto was always to keep swinging." He wasn't just talking about baseball. He was talking about life. When the world throws you a curveball of hate, you keep on swinging.

- **Dignity in the face of disgrace:** While others were losing their minds with anger and fear, Aaron stayed calm and focused. He answered the hate mail with class, kept showing up to work, and let his actions speak louder than any insult.

- **More than a number:** Breaking that record wasn't just about baseball. It was a home run for the civil rights movement. It showed that excellence knows no color, and that talent can't be confined by prejudice.

Aaron's legacy? It's bigger than baseball. He showed us all what real strength looks like. Not just the strength to hit a ball over a fence, but the strength to stand tall when the world's trying to knock you down.

- He opened doors for players of color, showing that they belonged in America's pastime.

- He became a voice for civil rights, using his fame to fight for equality off the field.

- He inspired a generation to dream big, to swing for the fences in life, no matter what obstacles stand in the way.

So, when you're facing your own impossible challenge, remember Hank Aaron. Remember the man who hammered through hatred, who swung his way into history, and who showed us all that the game—whether it's baseball or life—is there to be changed.

Now that's what we call a true game changer.

Kim Ng—A New League of Her Own

We're about to meet a real game-changer, someone who didn't just play ball—she rewrote the rulebook. Ladies, gents, and sluggers, put your hands together for Kim Ng!

Now, picture this: It's November 13, 2020. The sports world is buzzing like a beehive that's been whacked with a baseball bat. Why? Because Kim Ng just shattered a ceiling so high, it was practically in orbit. She became the first woman ever to be named General Manager of a Major League Baseball team. And let me tell you, getting there? It wasn't exactly a smooth ride around the bases.

Let's break it down:

- **The journey:** Ng's path to the top? It was like trying to steal home with the entire opposing team staring you down.

  o **Started as an intern with the Chicago White Sox in 1990:** Kim kicked off her career at the grassroots level, diving headfirst into the world of baseball. As an intern, she soaked up knowledge like a sponge, learning the ins and outs of the game from the ground up. This wasn't just a job; it was the start of a lifelong dream.

o **Became the youngest Assistant General Manager in MLB at 29:** Fast forward to 2001, and Ng wasn't just in the game; she was making waves. At just 29, she snagged the title of Assistant GM with the New York Yankees. This role didn't come easy, but it showcased her talent and determination, proving that age is just a number when you're driven by passion and skill.

o **Interviewed for GM positions at least five times before landing the big job:** Talk about perseverance! Ng faced rejection more times than a rookie striking out. Each interview was a chance to show what she was made of, and even when doors closed, she didn't let that keep her from stepping up to the plate again.

o **Spent 30 years climbing the ladder, rung by grueling rung:** Ng's journey was a marathon, not a sprint. Every position she held—from scouting to player development—added layers to her experience. She wasn't just waiting for the big break; she was building a foundation that would support her future success.

• **The hurdles:** Being a woman in baseball's boys' club? It's like trying to hit a knuckleball—tricky, unpredictable, and enough to make your head spin.

o **Faced skepticism about her knowledge of the game (Spoiler alert: She knows her stuff!):** Doubt was a constant companion, with critics questioning whether she had the chops to succeed in a male-dominated sport. But Ng silenced the naysayers with her expertise, proving time and again that her knowledge of the game was second to none.

- o **Dealt with the "old boys' network" that often overlooks talented women:** Navigating the traditional networks of baseball was no easy feat. The "old boys' club" often sidelined capable women, but Ng wasn't one to be overlooked. She fought for her place at the table, showcasing her skills and determination at every opportunity.

- o **Encountered stereotypes and biases at every turn:** Ng faced biases that ran deep, from assumptions about her abilities to outdated views on what a GM should look like. Each stereotype was a hurdle she had to leap over, and she did so with grace and grit, turning obstacles into stepping stones.

- **The climb:** Ng didn't just sit in the dugout waiting for her turn. She stepped up to the plate again and again.

- o **Worked in baseball operations for the White Sox, Yankees, and Dodgers:** With a resume that reads like a who's who of baseball, Ng gained invaluable experience working with some of the most prestigious teams in the league. Each role sharpened her skills and expanded her network, setting her up for future success.

- o **Served as MLB's Senior Vice President of Baseball Operations:** In this position, Ng wasn't just a spectator;

she was a key player in shaping the future of the league. Her decisions impacted teams and players alike, proving she could thrive at the highest levels of the sport.

- Built a reputation as a sharp negotiator and savvy talent evaluator: Ng's keen eye for talent and sharp negotiation skills made her a formidable force in the industry. She didn't just find players; she built winning teams, always looking for that next hidden gem.

- Learned every aspect of the game, from player development to contract negotiations: Ng's dedication to understanding all facets of baseball made her an invaluable asset. She immersed herself in every detail, ensuring she was well-equipped for whatever challenges lay ahead.

- Breaking through: When Ng finally got the call to the big leagues as GM, it wasn't just a win for her—it was a grand slam for women everywhere.

- Became the first woman GM in MLB history: This wasn't just a personal victory; it was a watershed moment in sports history. Ng's achievement paved the way for future generations of women in baseball, proving that the sky's the limit when you break barriers.

- Also the first Asian American GM in MLB history (talk about a double play!): Ng's impact goes beyond gender; she represents diversity in a sport that has often lacked it. Her success serves as a beacon of hope for aspiring athletes of all backgrounds, showing that anyone can reach for the stars.

- Opened doors for women in all sports, not just baseball: Ng's story isn't confined to the baseball diamond. Her groundbreaking role as GM has inspired women across all sports, demonstrating that with tenacity and talent, they can shatter glass ceilings and redefine what's possible.

Now, let's talk about what makes Kim Ng a true MVP:

- **Persistence:** Ng didn't quit after a few "no's." She faced rejection more times than a rookie swinging for the fences—but she kept stepping up to the plate until she hit it out of the park.

- **Expertise:** This isn't just a passion project for her; Ng knows every stat, strategy, and scenario. She consistently proved she was the sharpest person in any room, mastering every aspect of the game.

- **Thick skin:** You think striking out feels bad? Every time she faced doubt, discrimination, or another barrier, Ng didn't flinch. She brushed off the noise and stayed laser-focused on the win.

- **Passion:** Ng's love for baseball wasn't just a spark. Ng's dedication to baseball runs deep. It wasn't just a job or hobby—it was her life's mission, and that unwavering passion carried her through every challenge.

- **Trailblazing spirit:** She wasn't content with just making it to the show. Ng wanted to change the game for everyone coming up behind her.

Here's the thing, folks: Kim Ng didn't just break the glass ceiling —she smashed it into a million pieces and used them to make a disco ball. She showed the world that baseball isn't just a man's game. It's everyone's game.

So, what can we learn from Ng's journey to the top?

- **Dream big:** Don't let anyone tell you what you can't do. Ng dreamed of a job that no woman had ever held before—and she made it happen.

- **Know your stuff:** Whatever field you're in, be the expert. Know it inside and out, upside down, and backward.

- **Persevere:** Rejection isn't the end—it's just a pit stop on the road to success. Keep pushing, keep trying, keep believing.

- **Be a team player:** Ng didn't make it to the top alone. She built relationships, earned respect, and created a network of supporters.

- **Change the game:** Don't just play by the rules—rewrite them. Show the world what's possible when you refuse to be limited by stereotypes.

Kim Ng's story isn't just about baseball. It's about breaking barriers, chasing dreams, and changing the world. It's about looking at a field dominated by one group and saying, "Hey, I belong here too."

So, next time someone tells you "That's not for girls" or "You don't look like you belong here," remember Kim Ng. Remember the woman who stepped up to the plate, swung for the fences, and knocked it out of the park.

Lesson—Resilience and Pioneering Spirit

We've just witnessed two incredible stories of grit, determination, and straight-up awesomeness. Now it's time to break down the game tape and see what we can learn from these all-stars of barrier-breaking.

First things first: What's this resilience and pioneering spirit we're talking about?

- **Resilience:** Think of yourself as a supercharged bouncy ball. Every time life throws you to the ground—whether it's a tough day at school, losing a game, or not getting what you wanted—you don't just stay down. Nope! It's the ability to take a hit and keep on swinging. That's resilience—no matter how many times you fall, you always get back in the game.

- **Pioneering spirit:** Imagine you're an explorer in a video game, and everyone else is sticking to the same boring path. But not you. You're the one who thinks, "Wait a minute, what if I go this way?" That's pioneering spirit—having the courage to try something totally new, even when everyone else says, "But it's never been done before." You see an obstacle, and instead of following the crowd, you say, "I'm going to figure out a new way around it." It's all about daring to do something different, and maybe even discovering something awesome that no one else saw.

Now, how did Hank Aaron and Kim Ng show us what these look like in action? Let's break it down:

- **Hank Aaron's Resilience Playbook:**

  ○ Faced racist threats? Kept his cool and let his bat do the talking.

  ○ Pressure of breaking Babe Ruth's record? Handled it like a pro, one swing at a time.

  ○ Doubters said he couldn't do it? Proved them wrong with every home run.

- **Kim Ng's Pioneering Gameplan:**

  ○ Told baseball was a "man's world"? Said "Watch me" and climbed to the top.

  ○ Passed over for GM jobs? Kept swinging, interview after interview.

  ○ No female role models in MLB management? Became a role model herself.

Your Turn, Champ

So, how can you develop your own resilience and pioneering spirit? Glad you asked! Here's your training regimen:

- **Set big goals:** Don't just aim for a base hit—swing for the fences! We're talking home runs, not just base hits! Don't just aim for what's easy—go after that HUGE dream that makes your heart race.

  a. Write down your wildest dreams. Make them so big they scare you a little. You can use the SMART goal method and make it as fun as baseball! Here's and example, give it a go:

i. S – Specific: You can't just say, "I want to hit the ball." You've got to say where you want to hit it! Aim for a home run to the left field, or maybe a bunt that gets you on base. Your goals need details. Instead of "I want to be good at math," say "I want to get an A in my next math test."

ii. M – Measurable: In baseball, you track your hits, runs, and stats to know how you're doing. Your goals should be the same! Set something you can measure, like "I'll practice pitching for 20 minutes every day" or "I'll learn five new facts about space each week."

iii. A – Achievable: Just like in baseball, you don't swing for the fence if you're holding a toothpick instead of a bat. Set goals that stretch you, but are still possible. For example, if you want to be an artist, start by mastering one new drawing skill a month instead of expecting to paint the Mona Lisa next week.

iv. R – Relevant: In baseball, you focus on hitting, running, and catching because that's the game. Your goal has to make sense for you and what you care about! Don't set a goal to climb Mount Everest if your dream is to become a baseball star. Make sure your goal connects with your big dreams.

v. T – Time-bound: Baseball has nine innings, not infinity innings. Give yourself a deadline! If you want to finish a book or learn a new skill, set a timeline, like "I'll finish this by the end of the month" or "I'll learn 10 new vocabulary words by Friday."

- **Embrace the strikeouts:** Failure isn't the end—it's just part of the game. Let's try something different—how about "Failure Bounce-Back Drills"? It's a super cool method to embrace those strikeouts and bounce back even stronger. Here's your step-by-step guide to getting started:

  a. **Call a time-out:** After something goes wrong—whether it's a missed shot, a bad grade, or a failed attempt at anything—take a time-out. Like a coach calling a break after a tough inning, stop and breathe. This isn't the end of the game, just a chance to regroup!

  b. **Replay the moment:** Imagine you're watching the highlight reel of your life (you know, the one where you're the star). Replay what happened in your mind like a game recap. What went wrong? Did you lose focus? Was the problem too tough? This helps you see it clearly without all the emotions getting in the way.

  c. **Coaching tips:** Talk to your "coaches"—this could be a friend, teacher, or even your parents. Ask them for advice on what you could do better next time. Just like a baseball coach gives pointers after a bad swing, your coaches can help you see where you can improve.

  d. **Draw up a new game plan:** Now it's time to strategize! What can you do differently next time? Did you study enough? Could you try a different technique? Write down two or three things you'll change for your next try. This is your personal comeback plan—like switching your batting stance to knock that ball out of the park!

e. **Practice your bounce-back moves:** Just like you practice swinging the bat until you get it right, keep practicing your new plan. Didn't hit the mark in math? Try a different study trick. Didn't score that goal in soccer? Practice aiming! Every failure is just a drill for your next big success. Keep showing up, keep practicing, and soon you'll be hitting home runs.

f. **Celebrate progress:** The first time you get it right after a failure—throw yourself a mini-party! You don't have to wait until you're perfect. Every small win counts. Maybe it's extra ice cream, maybe it's a victory dance in your room, but celebrate how far you've come.

- **Train your mind:** Mental toughness is just as important as physical skills.

a. Practice positive self-talk. When things get hard, tell yourself, "I've got this!" Stand in front of the mirror and practice saying it out loud. You are your own hero, and even heroes need pep talks. Fill your head with good vibes, and soon enough, you'll start believing it!

- **Find your team:** Surround yourself with supporters who believe in you.

a. Identify your "Dream Team"—friends, family, mentors who have your back. But, let's take it up a notch with the idea of building your "Personal All-Star Panel"—because even the best players have mentors, coaches, and role models who inspire them to keep swinging for the fences:

i. Pick your MVPs: Start by listing people who totally inspire you. Think of it like drafting players for your dream team. Who do you look up to? It could be your favorite teacher, a friend who's always got your back, or a family member who gives the best pep talks.

ii. Follow the leaders: For the pros, start following their content regularly. Subscribe to their podcasts, YouTube channels, or social media posts. Make a list of your favorite ones, and check in with them daily or weekly.

iii. Mix reality with virtual inspiration: It's awesome to have both real-life mentors and virtual ones. Reach out to your teacher for advice, and also listen to that podcast that always pumps you up. You get the best of both worlds—real-world support and online wisdom!

iv. Create your "playbook": Start a notebook or a digital file where you jot down tips, advice, or quotes that hit home. It's like your personal playbook for life. Whether it's something a friend said or advice from a podcast, keep all that inspiration in one place to revisit when you need it.

v. Regular huddles: Just like teammates need practice, you need regular check-ins with your mentors and inspirational sources. Have weekly "huddles" with your Dream Team—this could be a lunch with a friend, a heart-to-heart with a parent, or even a chat with a teacher after class. For your virtual mentors, set a time each week to watch their latest posts or listen to their podcasts while taking notes.

vi. Share the wins: Share your progress with your Dream Team. Got a good grade after some tough studying? Tell them! Finished that tough project? Celebrate with them! Let your mentors and friends know how their support helped you knock it out of the park.

- **Stay curious:** Always be learning, always be growing.

  a. Try something new each week. It could be as small as trying a new hobby, reading a different type of book, or learning how to juggle! These little things add up and keep your brain in adventure mode.

- **Stand tall:** Don't let others define you or limit what you can do. You get to decide that.

  a. Come up with a personal mantra, like a secret code that reminds you of how awesome you are. Maybe it's, "I'm stronger than I think," or "I can do hard things." Write it down, say it often, and wear it like armor every time you face a challenge.

Taking It Beyond the Diamond

Now, let's take this off the baseball diamond and into your world. How can you use these lessons when life throws you a curveball?

- **Scenario 1: You're the only girl interested in joining the school's robotics club.**

  o **Channel your inner Kim Ng:** Show up like a boss. Just like Kim did in a male-dominated sport, you walk into that robotics room like you own it. Don't just be part of the club, dominate the club. Do your research, practice coding, and know your robot inside out. When they see your skills in action, any doubts will vanish faster than a homer flying over the outfield.

o **Be a pioneer:** Remember, you're not just joining a club— you're blazing a trail for every other girl who's secretly thinking about joining but is too nervous. When they see you in there, they'll realize that they can do it too. You're basically opening the gates to a whole new generation of girl engineers. Be that spark!

- **Scenario 2: You're facing racial stereotypes in your community.**

o **Take a page from Hank Aaron's book:** Stay dignified, stay focused, and let your actions do the talking. Whether it's excelling in academics, art, or sports, prove to everyone that stereotypes are garbage. Hank Aaron didn't shout back at his haters—he just kept hitting home runs. You do the same: let your achievements speak for themselves, and they will drown out the noise.

o **Be resilient:** Other people's opinions don't define you— YOU define you. When someone throws a prejudice your way, don't let it stick. Bounce back like that human bouncy ball, because their limited thinking doesn't even scratch the surface of your unlimited potential.

- **Scenario 3: You're told you're "not athletic enough" to try out for a sports team.**

o **Embrace the challenge:** Use those words as fuel. If someone says you can't prove them wrong. Hit the gym, practice daily, or find a sport that matches your passion.

Whether it's soccer, basketball, or even fencing, take it as a personal challenge to show them that your athleticism isn't up for debate.

Pioneer a new path: If traditional sports aren't your thing, no worries—invent your own game. There are sports like parkour, dance battles, or ultimate frisbee that don't need you to fit into anyone's box. Find what makes you feel strong and create your own version of being an athlete.

- **Scenario 4: You Bombed a Big Test, and Now You're Feeling Like You're Not "Smart Enough"**

  o **Embrace the strikeouts:** So, you failed a test? Big deal! That's just part of learning. What matters is what you do next. Instead of getting down, ask your teacher for help, hit the books harder, and study smarter. Like a player reviewing game tapes, figure out what went wrong and tackle it head-on. Next time? You'll ace it.

  o **Pioneer your study routine:** Maybe cramming all night isn't your style. No problem! Try something different. Create your own method of studying—maybe it's using flashcards, or turning your notes into a game, or even teaching the material to your dog (hey, if they sit through it, you know you've got it down!). Tailor your study style to match your brain's game plan.

- **Scenario 5: You Feel Like You Don't Fit In With Your Friend Group Anymore**

  o **Channel your resilience:** Friendships change, and that's okay. If you feel like an outsider, use that feeling to discover more about yourself. Maybe it's time to explore new interests or meet new people. The important thing is not to let it bring you down. You're not benched—you're just finding a new team that's better suited for you.

- o **Pioneer new friendships:** Seek out friends who share your new hobbies, whether it's in drama club, coding, sports, or a book club. Being a pioneer doesn't just apply to breaking barriers—it also means creating connections where they didn't exist before. Put yourself out there, join new groups, and forge new friendships.

Here's the deal: You've got the power to change the game, whatever your "game" might be. Maybe you'll be the first in your family to go to college. Maybe you'll invent the next big thing in technology. Or maybe you'll be the one to finally get pineapple accepted as a legitimate pizza topping (okay, that might be too far).

The point is, you've got a pioneering spirit inside you. You've got the resilience to bounce back from anything life throws your way. And you've got the power to make a difference.

Time for Some Self-Reflection

So, here's your homework:

1. **Identify your field:** What's the "game" you want to change?

1. **Spot the barriers:** What obstacles stand in your way?

1. **Plan your play:** How can you use resilience and a pioneering spirit to overcome these barriers?

1. **Make your move:** Take one small step today toward your goal.

Every game-changer started somewhere. Hank Aaron began by picking up a bat. Kim Ng started as an intern. You're starting by reading this book and dreaming big.

So, what are you waiting for? The world is your diamond, and you're up to bat.

Who knows? Maybe one day, we'll be writing a chapter about you.

CONCLUSION

We're rounding third and heading for home! This is it—the bottom of the ninth, bases loaded, and you're up to bat. Everything we've talked about, all the incredible stories we've shared, it all comes down to this.

So let's knock it out of the park!

When we first stepped onto this field of dreams? We've been on one heck of a journey, haven't we? We've seen underdogs become legends, watched ordinary people do extraordinary things, and learned that baseball isn't just a game—it's a masterclass in life.

"Sure, these stories are cool, but what's it got to do with me? I'm not exactly swinging for the major leagues here."

Well, hold onto your baseball caps, because here's the curveball —everything we've learned? It's not just about baseball. It's about you, your life, and how you play the game.

Let's take a quick trip around the bases and recap what we've learned:

- **First base:** Overcoming adversity. Life's gonna throw you some wild pitches, but it's how you handle them that counts. Remember Hank Aaron? The man faced death threats and still kept swinging. That's the kind of grit we're talking about.

- **Second base:** The importance of practice. You think Babe Ruth woke up one day and could hit homers in his sleep? Nope! It took hours, days, years of practice. Same goes for anything you want to be good at. Put in the work, and watch yourself improve.

- **Third base:** Teamwork and leadership. Baseball's not a one-man show, and neither is life. Learn to work with others, to lead when it's your turn, and to support your teammates. Remember, even the best pitcher needs a good catcher.

- **Sliding into home:** Handling pressure, learning from failure, and breaking barriers. These are the skills that separate the good from the great. Life's going to test you, knock you down, and tell you "no." But like Kim Ng, you've got to keep stepping up to the plate, no matter how many times you strike out.

Now, here's the really cool part—all these lessons? They're like the different pitches in a pro's arsenal. They work together, building on each other to make you unstoppable. Overcoming adversity makes you better at handling pressure. Practice helps you learn from failure. Teamwork and leadership? They're your secret weapons for breaking barriers.

So, how do you take all this and apply it to your life? Here's your game plan:

- **Identify your Field:**

  First, figure out where you want to shine. What are you passionate about? What's that one thing that lights a fire under you? Whether it's making the school team, mastering a subject that feels like a mountain right now, or learning to stand up for yourself in tough situations, this is your playing field. This is where you're going to pour your energy. Take a moment to visualize it. Can you see yourself standing tall, feeling confident in that area? That's your goal. Maybe it's sports, academics, or personal growth—whatever it is, it's the field where you'll focus your efforts. Identifying your field is crucial because it helps you channel your energy into a clear direction instead of spreading yourself thin. Once you know what game you're playing, you'll have a clearer sense of purpose, and every step forward will feel more intentional.

- **Practice, Practice, Practice:**

  You've heard the saying, "Practice makes perfect," right? Well, it may not always make things perfect, but it sure makes them better! Whatever goal you're aiming for, there's no shortcut around hard work. Set aside time each day to get better at your craft. The beauty of practice is that it builds over time. If you're starting from scratch, don't worry. Begin small, even if it's just 15 minutes a day. Soon enough, you'll find yourself increasing that time without even realizing it. Consistency is the secret ingredient to success. Just like an athlete trains their body, you're training your mind and skills. And don't forget, every time you practice, you're getting a little closer to your goal. Every small win adds up, and soon, you'll look back and be amazed at how far you've come. The key is to keep showing up, no matter how daunting it may seem at first.

- **Build your Team:**

Success isn't a solo mission. You need a solid support system to help you navigate through the challenges. Think of your team as your personal cheering squad, coaches, and sometimes even the ones who give you a reality check when you need it. These are the people who will celebrate your wins with you, pick you up when you're feeling down, and give you advice when you're stuck. Look around—friends, family, teachers, mentors—there are people in your life who can offer the guidance and support you need. Don't be afraid to reach out to them. Remember, even the best athletes have coaches and teammates who push them to their limits and believe in them. You don't have to do this alone, and having a strong team around you can make all the difference.

- **Embrace the Curveballs:**

Life is unpredictable, and that's okay. In fact, those unexpected twists and turns are what make the journey interesting. When life throws a curveball at you, don't run from it. Instead, face it head-on and learn from the experience. Every setback is an opportunity for growth. Challenges force you to stretch beyond your comfort zone, and that's where real growth happens. Think of these moments as tests of your resilience. How you respond to difficulties is what truly shapes your character. Instead of getting frustrated, look at each challenge as a lesson in disguise. The next time you're knocked off balance, remember: you're not being derailed, you're being refined.

- **Keep Swinging:**

Failure is a part of success. Even the greatest players don't hit a home run every time they step up to the plate. The secret is to keep swinging, no matter how many times you miss. Babe Ruth, one of the most famous baseball players in history, struck out over a thousand times, but he's remembered for his home runs. Why? Because he didn't let the failures stop him. He kept going. The same applies to you. Don't let a few setbacks stop you from pursuing your dreams. Keep pushing, keep swinging, and eventually, you'll hit your stride. Resilience is key. The more you bounce back from failure, the stronger you become. Keep that in mind as you move forward, and never be afraid to take another shot. You never know when your next swing will be the one that knocks it out of the park.

- **Break Barriers:**

Breaking barriers is all about challenging the obstacles in your path—whether they're personal doubts or societal expectations. Start by identifying what holds you back, then craft strategies to overcome those hurdles. Remember, every time you push against a barrier, you're not just changing your life; you're paving the way for others.

Remember, just like in baseball, life is a game of inches. You're not going to hit a grand slam every time, and that's okay. The key is to keep stepping up to the plate, keep swinging, keep trying. Every pitch is a new opportunity. And hey, we've loved having you in our dugout for this adventure. But now it's your turn to step up to the plate. Take what you've learned here and go change the game—your game.

Before you go, though, we've got one last favor to ask, let us know what you thought of the book. Love it? Tell us why! Think we struck out somewhere? Let us know! Your feedback helps us keep improving, just like a player watching game tapes.

So, what do you say? Are you ready to play ball? The game of life is waiting, and guess what? You're the star player. Now get out there and show 'em what you've got!

Play ball!

REFERENCES

A Coach's Reference Guide to Baseball Fundamentals. (n.d.). In *Hopkins Area Little League*. https://cdn3.sportngin.com/attachments/document/0027/8428/HALL_Coaches_Reference_Guide_to_Baseball_Fundamentals.pdf

Abdulaziz Almatari. (2023, November 3). *The power of consistency: A key to success in life*. Medium; Medium. https://medium.com/@MatariOfficial/the-power-of-consistency-a-key-to-success-in-life-84c56ca39d7a

Acocella, N. (2020). *Ruth changed the game forever*. ESPN. http://www.espn.com/sportscentury/features/00242487.html

Acquavella, K. (2021, January 22). *Hank Aaron's legacy will always be bigger than baseball thanks to his fight for civil rights*. CBSSports.com. https://www.cbssports.com/mlb/news/hank-aarons-legacy-will-always-be-bigger-than-baseball-thanks-to-his-fight-for-civil-rights/

Admin. (2017, August 27). *Ted Williams swing | The science of hitting*. Hitterish. https://www.hitterish.com/single-post/ted-williams-swing-analysis

Bergland, C. (2011, December 26). *The neuroscience of perseverance*. Psychology Today. https://www.psychologytoday.com/intl/blog/the-athletes-way/201112/the-neuroscience-perseverance

Blahous, C. (2024, March 28). *What baseball teaches us*. Discoursemagazine; Discourse. https://www.discoursemagazine.com/p/what-baseball-teaches-us

Caredda, S. (2019, November 21). *Build your Skills: Resilience*. Medium; The Intentional Organisation. https://medium.com/the-intentional-organisation/build-your-skills-resilience-84a963802900

Castrovince, A. (2021, January 23). *Facing racism, Aaron still had hope, optimism*. MLB. https://www.mlb.com/news/hank-aaron-overcame-racism-hate-throughout-life

Chicago Cubs break the 108-year curse, win World Series over Cleveland Indians - CBS News. (2016, November 3). CBS News. https://www.cbsnews.com/news/chicago-cubs-break-108-year-curse-win-world-series-over-cleveland-indians/

Cottrell, S. (n.d.). *Setbacks: the seeds of future success*. Skills for Study. https://www.skillsforstudy.com/blog/setbacks-seeds-future-success

Crim, J. (2023, May 30). *Mental toughness in sports: the psychology of mindset*. Behaviour Institute. https://thebehaviourinstitute.com/mental-toughness-in-sports-the-psychology-of-mind-set/

Crouch, A. (2016, April 29). *Baseball's life lesson: The road to success is paved with failures.* LinkedIn. https://www.linkedin.com/pulse/baseballs-life-lesson-road-success-paved-failures-adam-crouch

Cubs history and timeline. (2017). Wrigleyville Sports. https://www.wrigleyvillesports.com/pages/history-of-the-chicago-cubs?srsltid=AfmBOoqh_2olWOf0SmMXwCW0ayt2n8l5-USU_ygjnvPEQNA8ysA9bJY8

Curse of the Bambino. (2022, May 9). Wikipedia. https://en.wikipedia.org/wiki/Curse_of_the_Bambino

De La Cruz, M., Zamarripa, J., & Castillo, I. (2021). The father in youth baseball: A self-determination theory approach. *International Journal of Environmental Research and Public Health, 18*(9), 4587. https://doi.org/10.3390/ijerph18094587

Dejanna, M. (2023, June 23). *Overcoming setbacks: A motivational speech to fuel your success.* Medium; Medium. https://medium.com/@michaeldejanna/overcoming-setbacks-a-motivational-speech-to-fuel-your-success-65c8219748a4

Delgado, C. E. (2017). *Failure as a proponent of success.* Baseball and Business. https://baseballandbusiness.com/failure-as-a-proponent-of-success/

Demeo, C. (2023). *#Shortstops: Hank Aaron's influence.* Baseball Hall of Fame. https://baseballhall.org/discover/Shortstops-Hank-Aaron%27s-influence

Derek Jeter stats, fantasy & news. (2019). MLB. https://www.mlb.com/player/derek-jeter-116539

Dhyaa Al-Deen Nabil. (2024, June 5). *Sports on personal adaptability and resilience.* World Opportunities - Works to Provide Access to Global Experiences to All; World Opportunities. https://world-opportunities.com/sports-on-personal-adaptability-and-resilience/

Editorial. (2024, June 29). *Understanding group dynamics in team sports for success.* Education Uplifted. https://educationuplifted.com/group-dynamics-in-team-sports/

Editors, H. com. (2009, November 24). *Hank Aaron breaks Babe Ruth's all-time home run record.* HISTORY. https://www.history.com/this-day-in-history/aaron-sets-new-home-run-record

Editors, H. com. (2021, November 3). *Chicago Cubs win first World Series title since 1908, snap "curse."* HISTORY. https://www.history.com/this-day-in-history/sports-curses-chicago-cubs-world-series

Edmonson, B. (2024, January 7). *How sports and politics intertwine to reflect and shape our society*. Medium. https://billedmonson.medium.com/how-sports-and-politics-intertwine-to-reflect-and-shape-our-society-69566778647a

Elias, R. (2011). Baseball and American foreign policy. *Transatlantica, 2 | 2011*(2). https://doi.org/10.4000/transatlantica.5478

Eva, A. (2022, January 4). *Six ways to find your courage during challenging times*. Greater Good. https://greatergood.berkeley.edu/article/item/six_ways_to_find_your_courage_during_challenging_times

Flaherty, D. (2018, October 25). *The 2004 Boston Red Sox make history*. OUAT Sports. https://ouatsports.com/2004-boston-red-sox-sports-history-articles/

Forbes Coaches Council. (2024, August 12). 15 Strategies for finding courage when facing life's challenges. *Forbes*. https://www.forbes.com/councils/forbescoachescouncil/2020/05/27/15-strategies-for-finding-courage-when-facing-lifes-challenges/

Francis, B. (n.d.). *Scientists explored secrets behind Ruth's epic 1921 season*. Baseball Hall of Fame. https://baseballhall.org/discover/scientists-explored-secrets-behind-ruths-epic-1921-season

Fuchs, A. H. (2023). *Babe Ruth sees a psychologist*. American Psychological Association. https://www.apa.org/monitor/2009/11/babe-ruth

Geher, G. (2023, September 27). *What exactly is courage?* Psychology Today. https://www.psychologytoday.com/us/blog/darwins-subterranean-world/202309/what-exactly-is-courage

Glanville, D. (2011, August 12). *MLB - Mariano Rivera's one pitch keeps hitters guessing*. ESPN; ESPN. https://www.espn.com/mlb/story/_/id/6857725/mlb-mariano-rivera-one-pitch-keeps-hitters-guessing

Gonzales, L. (2023, November 27). *7 Reasons why consistency is essential for success*. Medium. https://medium.com/@lester03g/7-reasons-why-consistency-is-essential-for-success-b68ecd783543

Guest Contributor. (2024, July 9). *Baseball basics: Mastering MLB fundamentals*. Bat Flips and Nerds. https://batflipsandnerds.com/2024/07/09/baseball-basics-mastering-mlb-fundamentals/

Harris, F. (2024, March 26). *Beyond the field: The transformative power of sports in education and life skills development*. Medium; Medium. https://medium.com/@franharris/beyond-the-field-the-transformative-power-of-sports-in-education-and-life-skills-development-521a895cd0e5

History of the Chicago Cubs. (2021, April 27). Wikipedia. https:// en.wikipedia.org/wiki/History_of_the_Chicago_Cubs

In a league of her own, Miami Marlins make history with first female general manager. (2020, November 14). CBS News; CBS Miami. https:// www.cbsnews.com/miami/news/miami-marlins-name-first-female-gm-mlb-history/

infielddad. (2008, June 26). *Fearing "failure" in baseball.* High School Baseball Web. https://community.hsbaseballweb.com/topic/fearing-failure-in-baseball

Jabr, F. (2021). Competitive response as a factor and measure of mental toughness in competitive athletes. *Publicationslist.org, 14*(6).

Jacobsen, K. (2014, May 8). *Overcoming cultural barriers in Major League Baseball.* The Temple 10-Q. https://www2.law.temple.edu/10q/overcoming-cultural-barriers-major-league-baseball/

Joe Maddon. (2024, March 8). Wikipedia. https://en.wikipedia.org/wiki/ Joe_Maddon

Joe Maddon | American baseball manager. (2024). In *Encyclopædia Britannica.* https://www.britannica.com/biography/Joe-Maddon

John, J. (2023, June 9). *Explore the 7 methods of breaking those barriers.* Medium; ILLUMINATION. https://medium.com/illumination/explore-the-7-methods-of-breaking-those-barriers-86cdb20fdf4

Jon, C. (2018, June 25). *Youth baseball and life lessons.* Spiders Elite. https:// spiderselite.com/2018/06/25/youth-baseball-and-life-lessons/

Kelly, O. (2023, October 17). *The winning attitude - How to be a valuable team player in baseball.* LinkedIn. https://www.linkedin.com/pulse/winning-attitude-how-valuable-team-player-baseball-owen-kelly

Kim Ng. (2023, April 6). Wikipedia. https://en.wikipedia.org/wiki/Kim_Ng

Kim, K. J., Chung, S. A., Lee, S. J., & Han, D. H. (2024). Temperamental and neuropsychological predictors for major league pro-baseball success. *Sports Health: A Multidisciplinary Approach, 16*(2), 213–221. https://doi.org/ 10.1177/19417381241227642

Levy, M. (2024, May 17). *Chicago Cubs | History, notable players, & facts.* Britannica. https://www.britannica.com/topic/Chicago-Cubs#:~:text=The%20Cubs%20play%20in%20the

Marc Carig/The Star-Ledger. (2011, September 20). *Yankees' Mariano Rivera is more than just his cutter*. Nj. https://www.nj.com/yankees/2011/09/yankees_mariano_rivera_is_more.html

Michael Smith Brown. (2024a, February 12). *Unlocking success: The power of effective baseball leadership*. Goral Baseball. https://goralbaseball.com/blog/effective-baseball-leadership/

Michael Smith Brown. (2024b, February 13). *Cracking the code: Mastering pressure situations in baseball*. Goral Baseball. https://goralbaseball.com/blog/handling-pressure-situations-in-baseball/

Michael Smith Brown. (2024c, February 14). *Unleashing the power of teamwork and leadership in baseball*. Goral Baseball. https://goralbaseball.com/blog/teamwork-and-leadership-in-baseball/

Moonshot (baseball). (2024). The ARMory. https://armorypitching.com/moonshot-baseball/

More, A. (2021, May 7). *Baseball as life lessons - A more perfect union*. Medium; Medium. https://mjwhidden.medium.com/baseball-as-life-lessons-f3893efcede6

Neal, M. A. (2024, April 9). *Hank Aaron's home run record meant everything years ago; It still does*. Medium. https://medium.com/@tnimixtape/hank-aarons-home-run-record-meant-everything-years-ago-it-still-does-by-mark-anthony-neal-7ee31e5e397b

Ötting, M., Deutscher, C., Schneemann, S., Langrock, R., Gehrmann, S., & Scholten, H. (2020). Performance under pressure in skill tasks: An analysis of professional darts. *PLOS ONE*, *15*(2), e0228870. https://doi.org/10.1371/journal.pone.0228870

Ozzy's Collectible Hub. (2024a, May 8). *Decoding the science of hitting: Lessons from Ted Williams*. Medium; Medium. https://medium.com/@ozzycollectiblehub/decoding-the-science-of-hitting-lessons-from-ted-williams-05b796252f23

Ozzy's Collectible Hub. (2024b, June 7). *Superduperstar Reggie Jackson: The legend of "Mr. October."* Medium; Medium. https://medium.com/@ozzycollectiblehub/superduperstar-reggie-jackson-the-legend-of-mr-october-b5bf0c482495

Ozzy's Collectible Hub. (2024c, August 21). *Ted Williams on the science of hitting: A masterclass from baseball's greatest hitter*. Medium; Medium. https://medium.com/@ozzycollectiblehub/ted-williams-on-the-science-of-hitting-a-masterclass-from-baseballs-greatest-hitter-821e566e346e

Pate, D. (n.d.). *Baseball leadership: A lesson in individual and team performance*. TBM Consulting. https://www.tbmcg.com/resources/blog/baseball-leadership-a-lesson-in-individual-and-team-performance/

Penny de Valk. (2021, July 8). *Are we there yet? How cultivating a pioneering spirit can push career frontiers for you and others*. LinkedIn. https://www.linkedin.com/pulse/we-yet-how-cultivating-pioneering-spirit-can-push-career-de-valk

Posnanski, J. (2017, October 17). *The mind of Maddon*. Medium; Joe Blogs. https://medium.com/joeblogs/the-mind-of-maddon-4cb5cc6ae793

Roychowdhury, D. (2023, June 13). *How to build resilience and adaptability in sport and exercise*. Dr Dev Roychowdhury. https://www.drdevroy.com/resilience-and-adaptability-in-sport-and-exercise/

Rudolph, S. (2020). *Courage, luck, action – what is a pioneering spirit made of?* Porsche Newsroom. https://newsroom.porsche.com/en/2020/company/porsche-panel-talk-pioneering-spirit-volkswagen-drive-forum-berlin-22729.html

Saidon, N. (2022, July 21). *Self-determination theory: What is it, and what does it mean (practically) for coaches?* Balance Is Better. https://balanceisbetter.org.nz/self-determination-theory-what-is-it-and-what-does-it-mean-practically-for-coaches/

Salcinovic, B., Drew, M., Dijkstra, P., Waddington, G., & Serpell, B. G. (2022). Factors influencing team performance: What can support teams in high-performance sport learn from other industries? A systematic scoping review. *Sports Medicine - Open*, 8(1). https://doi.org/10.1186/s40798-021-00406-7

Seminoles, S. (2022, February 1). *What important life lessons does baseball teach?* Schaumburg Seminoles. https://www.schaumburgseminoles.com/what-important-life-lessons-does-baseball-teach/

Siebers, P. (2022, May 4). *Fifty years of psychology: pioneering spirit and resilience*. Universonline.nl. https://universonline.nl/nieuws/2022/05/04/fifty-years-of-psychology-pioneering-spirit-and-resilience/

Siegle, K. (2024, April 4). *The 20-year anniversary of the Boston Red Sox' curse-breaking season*. MLB. https://www.milb.com/news/the-20-year-anniversary-of-the-boston-red-sox-curse-breaking-season

Southwick, S. M., Bonanno, G. A., Masten, A. S., Panter-Brick, C., & Yehuda, R. (2014). Resilience definitions, theory, and challenges: Interdisciplinary Perspectives. *European Journal of Psychotraumatology*, 5(1), 25338. https://doi.org/10.3402/ejpt.v5.25338

Sportsloverguide. (2024, September). *Mastering baseball: A comprehensive beginner's guide to rules, skills, and strategies.* Medium; Medium. https://medium.com/@sportsloverguide2023/mastering-baseball-a-comprehensive-beginners-guide-to-rules-skills-and-strategies-dca3792dabb7

Stezano, M. (2019, January 31). *Jackie Robinson's battles for equality on and off the baseball field.* HISTORY; A&E Television Networks. https://www.history.com/news/jackie-robinson-color-barrier-baseball

Team JOOLA. (2021, October). *Optimization of adaptability and resilience in sports and life.* JOOLA; JOOLA. https://joola.com/blogs/updates/optimization-of-adaptability-and-resilience-in-sports-and-life?srsltid=AfmBOoqvabzygk-453MUvJPOvWIFVJksIPVbFZKWT5WTBxkbHKc9Ky5h

Ted Williams. (2020, September 20). Wikipedia. https://en.wikipedia.org/wiki/Ted_Williams

The Captain (miniseries). (2022, October 11). Wikipedia. https://en.wikipedia.org/wiki/The_Captain_(miniseries)

Tian, S., Chen, S., & Cui, Y. (2022). Belief in a just world and mental toughness in adolescent athletes: The Mediating Mechanism of Meaning in Life. *Frontiers in Psychology, 13*(10.3389/fpsyg.2022.901497). https://doi.org/10.3389/fpsyg.2022.901497

Tigers, R. (2019, May 8). *A message for the baseball community; Understanding success in a game built on failure.* Medium. https://medium.com/@Rawlings_Tigers/a-message-for-the-baseball-community-understanding-success-in-a-game-built-on-failure-aa588702ab91

2004 Boston Red Sox season. (2022, March 26). Wikipedia. https://en.wikipedia.org/wiki/2004_Boston_Red_Sox_season

University of California. (2017). *SMART goals: a how-to guide.* https://www.ucop.edu/local-human-resources/_files/performance-appraisal/How%20to%20write%20SMART%20Goals%20v2.pdf

Wikipedia Contributors. (2018a, November 28). *Babe Ruth.* Wikipedia; Wikimedia Foundation. https://en.wikipedia.org/wiki/Babe_Ruth

Wikipedia Contributors. (2018b, December 25). *Baseball.* Wikipedia; Wikimedia Foundation. https://en.wikipedia.org/wiki/Baseball

Wikipedia Contributors. (2019a, September 11). *Reggie Jackson.* Wikipedia; Wikimedia Foundation. https://en.wikipedia.org/wiki/Reggie_Jackson

Wikipedia Contributors. (2019b, September 18). *Derek Jeter*. Wikipedia; Wikimedia Foundation. https://en.wikipedia.org/wiki/Derek_Jeter

Wikipedia Contributors. (2019c, October 18). *Mariano Rivera*. Wikipedia; Wikimedia Foundation. https://en.wikipedia.org/wiki/Mariano_Rivera

Wikipedia Contributors. (2019d, November 2). *2016 World Series*. Wikipedia; Wikimedia Foundation. https://en.wikipedia.org/wiki/2016_World_Series

Wikipedia Contributors. (2019e, November 14). *Baseball rules*. Wikipedia; Wikimedia Foundation. https://en.wikipedia.org/wiki/Baseball_rules

Wikipedia Contributors. (2020a, January 18). *Chicago Cubs*. Wikipedia; Wikimedia Foundation. https://en.wikipedia.org/wiki/Chicago_Cubs

Wikipedia Contributors. (2020b, January 31). *Hank Aaron*. Wikipedia; Wikimedia Foundation. https://en.wikipedia.org/wiki/Hank_Aaron

Wikipedia Contributors. (2024a, June 26). *Persistence (psychology)*. Wikipedia; Wikimedia Foundation. https://en.wikipedia.org/wiki/Persistence_(psychology)#:~:text=It%20describes%20an%20individual

Wikipedia Contributors. (2024b, July 31). *The Science of Hitting*. Wikipedia; Wikimedia Foundation. https://en.wikipedia.org/wiki/The_Science_of_Hitting

Witz, B. (2016, November 3). Cubs end 108-year wait for World Series title, after a little more torment. *The New York Times*. https://www.nytimes.com/2016/11/03/sports/baseball/chicago-cubs-beat-cleveland-indians-world-series-game-7.html

Yue, A. L. S. (2020, July 18). *What competitive sports taught me about resilience and mental toughness*. Medium. https://alexlohsengyue.medium.com/what-competitive-sports-taught-me-about-resilience-and-mental-toughness-31a99eb8208e

Image References

Freepik. (2024). *All images supplied by Freepik - Free Graphic resources for everyone.* Freepik. https://www.freepik.com/

Made in the USA
Las Vegas, NV
18 December 2024

14657325R00075